Praise for *Naming Neoliberalism*

"Rarely are critiques of neoliberalism followed by beautiful, constructive proposals for alternative ways to live. By giving us both, Clapp offers this book as a gift to the church. The converse is also true: it is important not only to identify the life-affirming work churches are called to do but also to help congregations name and understand the dominating power of our age. Only when we are clear about what the gospel frees us from and frees us for, Clapp well argues, may the church be a relevant witness against the power and principality of neoliberalism that opposes God's reign."

—Jennifer M. McBride, author of *Radical Discipleship: A Liturgical Politics of the Gospel*; associate professor of theology and ethics, McCormick Theological Seminary

"This concise and accessible analysis takes us beneath the fear, inequality, war, hunger, and environmental devastation of the present age and shows us how they operate. Rodney Clapp unpacks the ideologies that try to convince us that the world must be so and then offers resources from the Christian tradition to enact a more livable world. No one is more skilled at bridging the scholarly and pastoral contexts than Rodney Clapp."

—William T. Cavanaugh, DePaul University

"Let's be honest. As pastor of a politically split church, I am not looking for ways to introduce more politics into congregational life. In an age of tweets and squawking, I thirst for the peace of Christ. But after reading Rodney Clapp's *Naming Neoliberalism*, I also see how hungry and lonely I have been for some weight and wisdom from a spiritual tradition that is older, larger, and deeper than I am while wandering in this desert of culture wars. Somehow, Clapp uses a hot-button topic to model how to have a cool Christian conversation across the aisles of politics or pews. I would gladly introduce this book to my church members—for its sense of perspective but most of all for its contagious hope for a church where God is still speaking louder and more lovingly than the pundits."

—Lillian Daniel, senior pastor of First Congregational Church of Dubuque, Iowa; author of *Tired of Apologizing for a Church I Don't Belong To*

"Rodney Clapp has written a profoundly pastoral book that prophetically unmasks neoliberalism not only as a rival ethic to the church but as a rival theology. By telling the story of how neoliberalism came to seem not only plausible but necessary, Clapp empowers the reader to perceive where alternative community responses can be cultivated. Jesus's kingdom proclamation disarmed the powers and revealed a new, inbreaking reality. Clapp's book follows in that exalted tradition."

—Samuel Wells, vicar of St Martin-in-the-Fields

"If you sense that something seems wrong with current manifestations of US Christianity, with our economic inequality, and with our culture warring but naming it is not easy, then this book is for you. Clapp's *Naming Neoliberalism* is the best historical and theological analysis available to us of where we are, how we got here, and what might be done about it. From a history of enclosures to an examination of slavery, a journey through the Thatcherite and Reagan complete capitulation to neoliberalism, followed by the Clinton willing acquiescence and much more, Clapp traces the history of neoliberalism judiciously, carefully, and with theological insight. This book is a must-read for every thoughtful person and is even more important for those who are thoughtless."

—D. Stephen Long, Maguire University Professor of Ethics, Southern Methodist University

"Unnamed and unnoticed, an unholy power exerts enormous sway over every dimension of life all around the globe. Think of current apocalypses: massive and ever-growing economic disparity, financial markets that no one understands, thousands of new refugees created every day, antidemocratic nationalisms and ethnic cleansing, environmental destruction and climate change. Rodney Clapp boldly names the destructive power at work in all of these: neoliberalism. Then, evermore boldly, he names the singular apocalypse of divine power and reality that puts neoliberalism to shame and calls us into renewed hope: the life, crucifixion, resurrection, and exaltation of Jesus Christ. This is a must-read for every pastor, professor, and student who wants to know our times and live faithfully in them."

—Douglas Harink, emeritus professor of theology, the King's University, Edmonton; author of *Resurrecting Justice: Reading Romans for the Life of the World*

"Rodney Clapp has provided another gift to the church—its pastors, leaders, and members—in this book. *Naming Neoliberalism* is a guidebook for navigating the contemporary political economy and its effects on culture, society, politics, and ethics; it looks back to the past in order to provide a wide-ranging yet understandable picture of the present. But do not be misled: as capable an introduction to contemporary capitalism as this book is, it is even more so a theological exploration of creation and covenant, human nature and sociability, and an example of Christian ethics done well. Crucially, he joins a richly layered picture of the church—a future-oriented community serving God's goal of creation and humanity fully restored and flourishing—to a sober description of the world made by unchecked capitalism and religious nationalism."

—Michael L. Budde, professor of Catholic studies and political science,
senior research professor, Center for World Catholicism
and Intercultural Theology (CWCIT), DePaul University

"In this biblically rich and astute book, Rodney Clapp exposes the obfuscating slipperiness of 'neoliberalism,' uncovers the roots of this disastrous vision of life, spiritually discerns its character, and unveils the abusive evil that it has unleashed on the most vulnerable in God's good creation. In stark contrast to this culture of death, Clapp evocatively and eloquently invites us into an apocalyptic vision of the new creation, embodied in welcoming communities of worship and hope, where justice is at home."

—Sylvia Keesmaat and Brian Walsh, coauthors of
Romans Disarmed: Resisting Empire, Demanding Justice

NAMING
NEOLIBERALISM

NAMING NEOLIBERALISM

Exposing the Spirit of Our Age

RODNEY CLAPP

Fortress Press
Minneapolis

NAMING NEOLIBERALISM
Exposing the Spirit of Our Age

Cover image: "Sofia" illustrated by Chloé Gray (2012)
Cover design: Brice Hemmer

Print ISBN: 978-1-5064-7265-2
eBook ISBN: 978-1-5064-7266-9

For Scott Young,
unafraid of doubt,
zestful and faithful in friendship
and engaging culture

We mean to suggest that the conflict between the neoliberal market and the Trinitarian God is over what reality is at its fundamental level. If reality is inconstant, inscrutable, with no discernible connection to justice (other than market rules), then a neoliberal order of class warfare, diminished substantial freedom, de-democratization, theaters of cruelty, accelerated environmental destruction, slum proliferation, mass incarceration, and mass deportation, at the very least, makes some sense. However, if reality is fundamentally love, mercy, and steadfast kindness, the crises of neoliberalism to which we have just pointed make no sense, and should be decried as false and, indeed, evil.

—Matthew T. Eggemeier and Peter Joseph Fritz,
Send Lazarus

CONTENTS

INTRODUCTION

Roundly commodified, made universally susceptible to pecuniary calculation, broken off from community and solidarity, captured comprehensively in a language only the market speaks—this is the plight of humanity, and indeed of the earth, in the age of neoliberalism.

Neoliberalism likes to go unnamed and so unnoticed. This book joins the growing chorus of voices who want that to be different. As chapter 2 will demonstrate, a host of activists, economists, historians, anthropologists, philosophers, and theologians have named and noticed neoliberalism. They know it is unique in the history of the world. And they know that it doesn't always act to the benefit of the world. Neoliberalism is the water we're swimming in—and too many are drowning in.

All authors believe in the power of articulation, or they wouldn't take the time and trouble to write. I write to raise the alarm, to expose the regnant ideology of our day. Though I've taken care to make this book respectable in the eyes of scholars who pick it up, I write especially for pastors and thoughtful laypersons who haven't had the leisure to examine and articulate for themselves just what neoliberalism is and just why it should be resisted. I hope this book will prompt sermons, inform Sunday school classes and adult education forum discussions, and challenge the imagination of the church on the ground in the dawning decades of the third millennium.

As will be clear soon enough, I see humans as social creatures all the way down. Sociology precedes psychology. And as a Christian, I affirm that the primary sociality that forms, animates, and directs believers is the church. But the church is not an end in itself. It exists for the sake of the world, just as God's salvation is about nothing less than all creation. The church's distinctiveness is nothing it possesses; rather, it is what it is possessed by. What the church is gripped by is not its own specialness or anything it can control or contain but instead the good news revealed or "apocalypsed" in the life and work of Jesus Christ.

Accordingly, that apocalypse is the wellspring of the church's mission and work in each particular time and place. In our time and place—in a world under the spell of neoliberal capitalism—such apocalyptic can be the basis of a resistance to and (we pray) the overcoming of a principality and power that is choking us and all creation to death. So as will become clear in chapter 3 and throughout the rest of the book, I am writing of apocalyptic not as imminent doom and gloom but as the throbbing heart of Christian faith and hope.

The economy or plan of this book is straightforward.

Chapter 1 tells the backstory of neoliberalism, of the liberalism and capitalistic modernity that begat it. Digging into the roots of neoliberalism, it introduces and probes the theme of freedom and notices that while we all want to be free *from* many things, we aren't at all sure what we are free *for*. A character in Jonathan Franzen's novel *Freedom* gives voice to this deep American ethos. "You may be poor," says the character, "but the one thing nobody can take away from you is the freedom to f—k your life up whatever way you want to."[1] This concern for not only freedom *from* but freedom *for* will set up the main body of the book (chapters 4–7), where chapters are

---

1. Franzen, *Freedom*, 361. For my review of the novel, see Clapp, "Free for What?"

titled and organized around both negative (from) and positive (for) freedom.

Chapter 2 turns directly to neoliberalism and seeks to portray it in its fullness and depth. I rely not only on scholars but also on filmmakers to sketch the political economy and cultural ethos that has captured our world. I end by suggesting that despite neoliberalism's almost incredible capacity to absorb and disarm threats to its regnancy, it faces certain immanent crises that may contribute to its downfall.

Chapter 3 morphs into the directly theological. It probes the heart of (especially Pauline) Christianity, arguing for an apocalyptic that reveals the true end (that is, goal) of history and hope of the world: Jesus the Christ who lived, died, and was resurrected on behalf of his creation. Using Emma Donoghue's extraordinary novel *Room*, I show how, in the light of apocalyptic, we live in a whole new creation—a creation that is not finally named by sin, death, or any principality and power.

Chapter 4 shifts into the apocalyptic engagement of neoliberalism that comprises the rest of the book. It argues for God's economy in contrast to the sprawling, tentacular, but actually less comprehensive economy of neoliberalism.

Chapter 5 takes up nationalism, a crucial prop of neoliberalism. It challenges a dominant narrative of the United States as the chosen nation and indeed a sort of church. That in turn leads into a discussion of politics and the ways the church both has and is a politics. In fact, since we live always at the behest of one or another political economy, chapters 4 and 5 are twins, and each should be read in tandem with the other.

Chapter 6 takes our eyes off primarily human concerns and considers the created world as a whole, which is also a part of God's redemptive work. It insists that theologically, humans have always been part of a wider ecological web, a web now desperately threatened by the human-induced climate crisis. It is in the climate crisis that neoliberalism's death-tending ways are revealed perhaps most dramatically, so any book engaging or intervening in neoliberalism must take account of it.

Chapter 7 concerns one power even neoliberalism cannot deny or claim to overcome: the certainty of death. Defining death in a trifold, apocalyptically influenced fashion as a separation from the constant source and sustainer of life—God—I explore how Christian hope defeats even this most fearful and implacable enemy. This is but one more way in which Christian apocalyptic grants a political economy that is wider, deeper, and richer than neoliberalism.

Finally, in the epilogue, I dare to gaze into the future and suggest further how an apocalyptically centered church may play a role in naming and taming neoliberalism and in surviving and thriving in its own mission—even in times of increased weakness (that is, without the propping up of government and culture), hyperpluralism, and Epicureanism, or the understanding that God is uninvolved with and no longer has anything to do with God's creation.

My hope is that even if you have never heard of the term *neoliberalism* before you picked up this strangely titled book, you will by its end have a clear sense of what it is. Once named, it is not hard to recognize and to see all around us. It indeed exercises a stupendous hegemony of our lives and of our imaginations. But I hope you will also see that neoliberalism, in the light of the gospel, need not be finally overpowering. In Paul's apocalyptic, we find the means to "be transformed by the renewing of your imaginations" (Rom 12:2, as we may fairly paraphrase him). It is only by such transformation that we may escape the suffocation, the drowning of neoliberalism, which surrounds and interpenetrates the workings of our present world like an amorphous and enormous octopus.

1

AFTER LIBERALISM

What are people? According to liberalism, people are first, foremost, and finally individuals. They are best understood and appreciated in distinction from any social or political ties they may have or that might bind, possess, grasp, or define them. They are constituted atomistically, apart from their families, countries, faith communities, classes, ethnicities, sexes, vocations, or places in the flow of history.

And what are people for? According to liberalism, individuals exist for freedom. The freedom that engages them is one of choice. They are to strive for autonomy, for liberating themselves from any external authorities (religions, ways of life, customs) that would place or constrain them. "Sapere aude!" cried the early liberal philosopher Immanuel Kant: "Think for yourself!"[1] The freedom liberalism seeks preeminently to guard is a negative freedom, a freedom *from* the interference of or dependence on others.

From roughly the seventeenth century until today, liberalism has developed as a political philosophy and way of life. Since it builds from the autonomous individual, liberalism has had both to ensure

1. More literally, "Know boldly!"

that individual freedom remains sacrosanct and to account for individuals acting communally—that is, politically. Its premier thinkers have sought to do so by positing the state as the agent that coordinates individual interests and rescues humanity from a war of all against all (Thomas Hobbes), by presenting and upholding the primacy of private property (John Locke), and by proposing that individuals sometimes find it in their interests to socially contract with one another (Jean-Jacques Rousseau).

How has liberalism brought its theories down to earth? Its politics have been enacted through the boots of soldiers, as with America's Revolutionary War (John Locke was easily the favorite philosopher of the Founding Fathers), and its economics have been realized through the work boots of men—and women and children—herded into its factories over the course of the Industrial Revolution. Liberalism has grown up alongside and in symbiosis with capitalism.

CAPITALISM IS NOT NATURAL

Ask the typical man or woman on the street about economics, and you will get the impression that capitalism is simply a natural phenomenon. Like a mushroom in loamy soil, it arose more or less benevolently, following the laws of nature. But capitalism did not spring into existence full blown as a glittering department store. Nor was it free of (debatable and hotly debated) human intention. It has a history. Recognizing this history means that we denaturalize capitalism. When we naturalize and see capitalism as purely a fact of nature, we place it beyond any criticism. A hurricane cannot be critiqued; it simply is, and humans affected by it can only respond to it as and after it happens. But recognizing that capitalism has a history opens it to both positive and negative criticism—and change.

"As Ursula Le Guin recently urged science fiction writers to consider, 'We live in capitalism. Its power seems inescapable. So did the divine right of kings.'"[2]

In England, where the Industrial Revolution centered, incipient capitalism needed laborers in great number. There was a problem. The English masses lived in largely self-sufficient communities, dependent on a commons. The commons consisted of pasture and forests shared by all who lived in the community. Livestock of various families grazed on the commons. Besides fodder for stock, pasture and forest provided fuel and bedding. Rural people larded their tables by hunting, fishing, and fowling in the shared countryside.

This is not to say markets didn't already exist. But they were small, supplemental, and embedded within the communities. The creation of an overarching market, what would come to be called the free market, with trade across (and beyond) the nation, was another matter. That required industrialization, dependent on manufactures and factories filled with workers. But the potential workers were not ready and willing to leave their community-based way of life for longer workdays and sparse compensation under another's employ. Put otherwise, the common men and women did not enter the "free" market freely.[3]

---

2. Davies, "Introduction," 22.

3. Nor was it only adults who were shoved into the industrial workforce. John Locke wanted labor to commence at the age of three. The liberal and utilitarian Jeremy Bentham advocated for age four, as did Archbishop William Temple. Perelman, *Invention of Capitalism*, 19 and 22. See also Cavanaugh, *Field Hospital*, 78: "The truth . . . is the separation of capitalists from wage laborers was accomplished with deliberate and shocking brutality. Coercion was necessary because no sensible person would voluntarily exchange a life of dignified subsistence for the dehumanization of the factory."

Flying in the face of their professed laissez-faire principles, classical political economists urged and achieved state intervention to push (potential) workers out of their small-scale economies into one overarching capitalist economy. By law and state force, the commons were broken up and enclosed. The gentry and other comparatively wealthy classes acquired pieces of what had been the commons and fenced them off. So much for the shared pastures where the ordinary families' cattle, sheep, goats, and pigs had grazed.[4]

And not only were the commoners denied pastures; they were also denied the forests. Beginning in 1671 and ranging into the nineteenth century, the game laws forbade hunting and fishing on gradually enclosed lands. Eventually, the game laws prohibited all but about 1 percent of the population from hunting. Here the interests of the gentry and capital coincided. The gentry could enjoy the prestige of hunting, with no interloping "poachers." Capitalists would benefit from crushing the potential subsistence living by the commoners, forcing the commoners to accept wage labor and file into the factories. As a journalist lamented in 1826, it was "difficult to make an uneducated man appreciate the sanctity of private property in game [when] . . . the produce of a single night's poach was often more than the wages of several weeks' work."[5]

Indeed, it was a bare and undignified subsistence level of life planned for these early working people. Various thinkers and activists were starkly clear that only poverty would thrust them into the factories, and ongoing poverty (though not outright starvation, which would of course eliminate workers) was their lot. The political economist Adam Smith estimated that "for one very rich man, there must be at least five hundred poor, and the affluence of

4. On enclosures, see Perelman, *Invention of Capitalism*, 13–22.
5. Cited in Perelman, 43. For the figures earlier in the paragraph, see 38 and 53.

the few supposes the indigence of many." As one Charles Hall put it in 1805, "If they were not poor, they would not submit to employments." Police magistrate Patrick Colquhoun, in 1815, elaborated: "Poverty is therefore a most necessary and indispensable ingredient in society, without which nations and communities could not exist in a state of civilization. . . . *It is the source of wealth*, since without poverty, there could be no labour; there could be *no riches, no refinement, no comfort*, and no benefit to those who may be possessed of wealth." To skip for a moment out of the English context, consider Benjamin Franklin's candid appraisal: "No man acquainted with political and commercial history can doubt [that] Manufactures are founded in poverty. It is the multitude of poor without land in a country, and who must work for others, at low wages or starve, that enables undertakers to carry on a manufacture." And again, more concisely, "Great Establishments of Manufacture require great Numbers of Poor to do the work for Small Wages."[6]

SLAVERY, THEFT, AND THE GROWTH OF CAPITALISM

What economic historians call the primitive accumulation of capital took centuries. It included not only the enclosures and game laws but outright violent force, as state agencies of the police and military quashed strikes and other means of resistance from the commoners.[7] Let us now leap an ocean and a couple of centuries to the nineteenth-century United States.

6. See Perelman, 214, 15, 23, 268, and 275, respectively.
7. Another facet of industrialization and capitalization, closely allied with the state, was improved gun technology and manufacturing and the related development of British imperialism. Historian Priya Satia comments that "the commonly

The institution of chattel slavery was based on three gross immoralities: kidnapping, torture, and theft. The kidnapping is obvious. Millions of Africans were abducted from their homes and removed to a distant country. The torture is both obvious and not so obvious. Its obviousness shows through the whips brandished on human beings, as if they were so much livestock. The less obvious—but no less profoundly real—torture requires reflecting on the mental anguish of people ripped from their homes, families, and cultures; denied their given names and languages; then mercilessly worked to an early death. This torture was the deprivation of a slave's past (home, family, name) and future (which was crushed by unremunerated, onerous labor—slaves called the cotton fields "hell without fires"[8]—and the ongoing separation of slave parents from their children).

Theft was the fundamental and encompassing immorality of slavery. Kidnapping, after all, is a form of theft. And the emotional, spiritual torture I have just mentioned was a theft of the slave's past and future. That slaves were not remunerated can be reasonably seen as a theft of (due) wages or wealth. The control or indisposition of the slaves' bodies and hopes was a theft of their very selves. So it

---

accepted story of the industrial revolution . . . is typically anchored in images of cotton factories and steam engines invented by unfettered geniuses. The British state has little to do with this version of the story. . . . But it is wrong: state institutions drove Britain's industrial revolution in critical ways." She shows that the state "did much more than minimalistically provide the financial and transportation infrastructure, as traditionally portrayed; it consumed metal goods [not least guns] in the mass quantities that made industrial revolution necessary and possible." And "much of the emerging economic order owed its existence to wars of imperial expansion" (*Empire of Guns*, 2, 6, 7).

8. Baptist, *Half Has Never Been Told*, 205.

is not for nothing that the slaves used the language of "stealing" to describe most basically what had happened to them.[9]

The massive theft that was slavery is the tainted wellspring of American capitalism. In the United States, capital—accrued for the wealthiest over generations—was built on the lacerated backs of Black people. To appreciate the magnitude of this, we must remember that cotton was the material center of the maturing Industrial Revolution. What oil and computerization are to our current economy, cotton was to the nineteenth-century industrial economy. As the historian Edward Baptist summarizes,

> In the span of a single lifetime after the 1780s, the South grew from a narrow coastal strip of worn-out plantations to a subcontinental empire. Entrepreneurial enslavers moved more than 1 million enslaved people, by force, from the communities that survivors of the slave trade from Africa had built in the South and in the West to vast territories that were seized—also by force—from their Native American inhabitants. From 1783 at the end of the American Revolution to 1861, the number of slaves in the United States increased five times over, and all this expansion produced a powerful nation. For white enslavers were able to force enslaved African-American migrants to pick cotton faster and more efficiently than free people. Their practices rapidly transformed the southern states into the dominant force in the global cotton market, and cotton was the world's most widely

9. See Baptist, 187–89. The historian Steve Fraser remarks, "Slavery was actually the ultimate form of primitive accumulation. The greatest fortunes of the era were amassed because slaves were forcibly dispossessed of everything they had or were born into that state of dispossession" (*Age of Acquiescence*, 107).

traded commodity at the time, as it was the key material during the first century of the industrial revolution.[10]

Baptist estimates that more than $600 million, almost half of the economic activity in the United States in 1836, rested directly or indirectly on the cotton market. And in the 1850s, southern cotton production doubled, from two million to four million bales. The world's consumption of cotton exploded from one and a half billion to two and a half billion pounds, some used in the US North and South but most going to western European factories.[11]

Note that the free North as well as the enslaving South were largely dependent on cotton production. In the North, cotton mills were established in and spread from Massachusetts and Rhode Island. "By 1832, . . . factories and workshops across the North employed about 200,000 workers. The biggest share was in cotton mills, which were the most mechanized, capital-heavy, *industrial* kind of industry in the entire United States." This new industry in turn created a new class, able and ready to spend on a range of items, including iron goods, ready-made clothes, rope, furniture, and shoes. Thus as of 1832, "cotton made by enslaved people was driving US economic expansion. Almost all commercial production and consumption fed into or spun out from a mighty stream of white bolls."[12]

Meanwhile, throughout the nineteenth century, slaves dramatically increased the amount of cotton they picked. For example, from 1805 to 1850 in Mississippi, the amount of cotton picked by the typical "hand" increased three, four, or six or more times over.

10. Baptist, *Half Has Never Been Told*, xxiii.
11. Baptist, 322 and 350.
12. Baptist, 318 and 319.

Across the newer southwestern slave states, from 1811 to the 1860s, there was a productivity increase of 361 percent.[13] What accounted for these incredible gains?

In a word, torture. Daily minimums were set for each slave. At the end of the day, the picking of each slave was weighed. Those who picked under the set (and over time, constantly rising) minimum were whipped, with the number of lashes calibrated to the amount they had fallen short. Of course, no one was eager to admit "that they lived in an economy whose bottom gear was torture."[14]

I rehearse the stories of enclosure, the game laws, and US slavery to indicate that liberalism and its concomitant capitalism did not arise naturally and benignly. Human intentionality and, more specifically, state oversight and (sometimes nakedly violent) force were crucial to capitalism's inception and growth. I made that explicit in recounting enclosure and the game laws. It hardly needs to be added that government was essential to the institution of and policing on behalf of slavery: making it legal, implementing and enabling the slave market, brutally punishing runaway slaves and their allies, and declaring, from the highest court in the land, that African American slaves were only three-fifths human.

If we are, as Jesus counseled, to be not only as innocent as doves but as shrewd and wise as serpents (Matt 10:16), we do well to ask of the free market, How and in what way is it free, and for whom is it free or freeing?[15] The elimination of legal slavery does not antiquate these questions. Still today, the wealth produced by the free market

13. Baptist, 126.

14. Baptist, 131–34, quotation 139.

15. *Freedom* can be and has under neoliberalism been recast "as the freedom to exploit, rather than exchange" (Davies, *Limits of Neoliberalism*, 51).

depends in no small part on sweatshop labor and the immiseration of millions in the majority world.

THE EARLY ENGAGEMENT OF CHRISTIANITY AND CAPITALISM

Telling the story of Christianity's engagement with capitalism requires glancing back to the Middle Ages. In this precapitalistic setting, markets were present and operative but bounded and channeled: "If this was an economy familiar with markets, it was also one which lacked the concept of a market order as a self-regulating system of economic relationships. . . . Contemporaries regarded economic activity as being subordinated to ethical ends. They assessed its legitimacy in terms of moral imperatives and their attitudes were both enshrined in their economic institutions and expressed in practice."[16]

Under the watchful eye and guidance of the church, trade was allowed but seen as inherently morally dangerous. Finance was "if not immoral, . . . at best sordid and at worst disreputable."[17] It was right for a man to seek wealth to the degree necessary for a livelihood in his station and business. But to seek more than the necessary was regarded as avarice, and avarice was a deadly sin. One was expected not to make profits more than the wages of his work and to carry profits into and for the public benefit. Private property was seen as "a necessary institution, at least in a fallen world. . . . But it

16. Keith Wrightson, quoted in Gregory, *Unintended Reformation*, 260.
17. Tawney, *Religion and the Rise*, 45. Tawney concludes provocatively: "The unpardonable sin is that of the speculator or middleman, who snatches private gain by the exploitation of public necessities. The true descendant of the doctrines of Aquinas is the labour theory of value. The last of the Schoolmen was Karl Marx" (48).

is to be tolerated as a concession to human frailty, not applauded as desirable in itself; the ideal—if only man's nature could rise to it—is communism."[18] Such an ideal—of course, decidedly not that of the later, state-directed communism of the Soviet Union and China—was represented by monasticism, where property was held in common.

In this religiously and ethically directed economy, the estate, of whatever degree of wealth, was, as the economic historian R. H. Tawney puts it, "somewhat encumbered. It must be legitimately acquired. It must be in the largest possible number of hands. It must provide for the support of the poor. Its use must as far as practicable be common." In short, for "the medieval thinkers . . . society is a spiritual organism, not an economic machine," and economic activity "is one subordinate element within a vast and complex unity, . . . to be controlled and repressed by references to moral ends for which it supplies the material means."[19]

The Protestant Reformers had largely similar attitudes, though significantly without the overarching, monocular guidance of the Roman Catholic Church, whose singular authority they rejected. Luther insisted that lending should be free, was against dealing in futures or investing in rent charges, and would refuse usurers the sacrament, absolution of sins, and Christian burial. Calvin taught that gathering interest on loans should be lawful but set caps on a maximum rate of interest. In addition, he thought loaning should be occasional, saw lending reprehensible as a regular occupation, and expected loans to be gratis to the poor.[20] Historian Brad Gregory summarizes, "The bottom line is clear: like radical

18. Tawney, 45.
19. Tawney, 45 and 73.
20. Tawney, 104 and 115.

Protestants, the magisterial reformers, including Calvin, unambiguously condemned avarice, acquisitive individualism, and any separation of economic behavior from biblical morality or the common good."[21]

Yet changes occurred, affecting behaviors and outcomes in the long term. Luther internalized charity and made the use of money more a matter of attitude and less a matter of outward behavior. He emphasized the doctrine of justification by grace through faith and stressed that a person's individual relationship with God—trusting in justification—was paramount. "Thus," Tawney writes, "the bridges between the worlds of the spirit and of sense are broken, and the soul is isolated from the society of men, that it may enter into communion with its Maker."[22] The focus shifted from Christians being a corporate, mutually responsible body of believers to individuals holding certain beliefs: "Since salvation is bestowed by the operation of grace in the heart, and by that alone, the whole fabric of organized religion, which had mediated between the individual soul and its Maker—divinely commissioned hierarchy, systematized activities, corporate institutions—drops away, as the blasphemous trivialities of a religion of works. . . . Man's actions as a member of society were no longer the extension of his life as a child of God: they were its negation."[23]

The early Anabaptists, on the other hand, held to a more embodied, corporate Christian ethic. Animated by a vision of communal

21. Gregory, *Unintended Reformation*, 268.

22. Tawney, *Religion and the Rise*, 105.

23. Tawney, 106–7. Relatedly, the historian John Bossy observes that the word *Christianity*, before the seventeenth century, signaled "a body of people." By and after the seventeenth century, it meant "an 'ism' or body of beliefs" (*Christianity in the West*, 171).

sharing, they subordinated economics to theology: "In the sixteenth century all Anabaptist groups were hostile to mercantile life and acquisitiveness, prizing manual labor and a materially humble way of life (as the Old Order Amish in North America continue to do today)."[24]

Meanwhile, less wary than the Lutherans of the constructive uses of the law, the Calvinists followed a different trajectory. The Calvinist aims not merely at personal salvation but at the glorification of God, the sanctification of the world that is meant to be a theater of God's goodness and supremacy. In this frame, good works do not attain salvation, yet they can be marks of assurance that it has been attained.

The Swiss Reformers saw thrift, diligence, sobriety, and frugality as Christian virtues. Though obsolescent in the world of twenty-first-century consumeristic capitalism, these very virtues were necessary for success in the world of early, burgeoning, production-oriented capitalism. And Calvin and later Reformed interpreters addressed their teaching primarily to men of affairs, those engaged in trade and industry, who comprised the most modern and forward-looking persons at a time when commercial civilization was more and more taken for granted.[25]

Concerned with nothing less than the sanctification of the world, the Calvinists, where in charge, constructed a panoptic oversight of their communities. Zwingli instituted excommunication for murder, theft, unchastity, perjury, and avarice. He also outlawed

---

24. Gregory, *Unintended Reformation*, 265.
25. Tawney cites a Puritan pamphleteer who wrote in 1671, "There is a natural unaptness in the Popish religion to business, whereas on the contrary among the Reformed, the greater their zeal, the greater their inclination to trade and industry, as holding idleness unlawful" (*Religion and the Rise*, 206).

mendicancy and entitled to poor relief no inhabitant who wore ornaments or luxurious clothes, played cards, or failed to attend church. In Geneva, Calvin drafted regulations for markets, crafts, buildings, and fairs. He instituted the control of prices, interests, and rents. In the later Puritan theocracy of New England, tobacco, immodest fashions, toasting with drinks, and buying cheap and selling dear were all forbidden. There they also regulated prices, limited interest rates, fixed a minimum wage, and whipped incorrigible idlers.[26]

If many of these restrictions (and their related punishments) now strike us as draconian, it is no surprise theocracy has had its day. In a pluralizing world, few if any communities remain pure (as in Puritan). Instead, the (Reformed) Protestant work ethic has over centuries been secularized and transmogrified. Hard work and attendant prosperity might formerly have served as assurances that one was among God's elect. In this sense, the Protestant ethic preceded and undergirded capitalism.[27] But gradually, the concern for election and salvation wore away. What was left was regnant capitalism, with a divorce of the market and inherited Christian morality. Lutherans, in many ways, turned inward and away from the discipline of the market. The Reformed, denied their theocracies, found themselves baptizing prosperity but also struggling to contain and discipline the market. Both segregated economic behavior from increasingly interiorized theological convictions.[28]

26. Tawney, 125, 123, 135, 136.
27. At least to the degree sociologist Max Weber was right in his classic *The Protestant Ethic*.
28. See Gregory, *Unintended Reformation*, 270–75.

THE STORY THAT WE HAVE NO STORY

This is exactly as liberalism, attendant to its handmaiden, capitalism, would have it. Liberalism divided life into public and private spheres. The state was the regnant coordinator of the public sphere, which supposedly hewed to universal human concerns and interests. Religion and morality, meanwhile, were relegated to the private sphere and focused on the individual. As John Locke proclaimed, in early and quintessentially liberal fashion, "All the life and power of true religion consist in the inward and full persuasion of the mind."[29]

Following suit, Friedrich Schleiermacher, the father of liberal theology, believed that "nothing remains as the immediate sphere of [God's] kingship but the inner life of men individually, and in their relation to each other." Similarly, the Lutheran theologian and church historian Adolf von Harnack declared, "The kingdom of God comes by coming to the individual, by entering into his soul and laying hold of it. True, the kingdom of God is rule by God; but it is the rule of the holy God in the hearts of individuals."[30]

As regards the privatization and individualization of faith, the evangelical trajectory is no different. While still reacting to liberalism's Social Gospel, today's evangelicalism is more individualistically focused than theological liberalism. For example, the evangelical New Testament scholar Douglas Moo, commenting in 1996 on the apostle Paul's seminal Letter to the Romans, stresses, "The bulk of Romans focuses on how God has acted in Christ to bring the *individual* sinner into a new relationship with himself (chaps. 1–4), to

---

29. Quoted in Cavanaugh, *Field Hospital*, 183.
30. Schleiermacher and Harnack, cited in Ziegler, *Militant Grace*, 39 and 40.

provide for that *individual's* eternal life in glory (chaps. 5–8), and to transform that *individual's* life on earth now (12:1–15:13)."[31]

Stanley Hauerwas, the piercing theological critic of liberalism, has something of this liberal Protestant-evangelical mirroring in mind when he alludes that Protestant liberalism and evangelicalism are the "same thing." Both are instantiations of Christianity that "reflect the formation of Christianity in modernity to be 'beliefs' adhered to by an 'individual.' Both are the bastard stepchildren of pietism run amuck."[32]

For further clarity, it behooves us to delve deeper into Hauerwas's critique of liberalism. In a 1981 essay entitled "The Church and Liberal Democracy: The Moral Limits of a Secular Polity," Hauerwas set forth in nuce a case on the fallacies of liberalism that he has subsequently and influentially unleashed throughout his prolific career. As I said at the beginning of this chapter, liberalism focuses on the atomistic individual, apart from the particular traditions and communities that form and inform actual individuals. Hauerwas quotes the economist Milton Friedman in declaring that "a major aim of the liberal is to leave the ethical problem for the individual to wrestle with."[33] In liberalism, says Hauerwas, "the individual is the sole source of authority. Thus Hobbes and Locke, to be sure in very different ways, viewed the political problem as how to get individuals, who are necessarily in conflict with one another, to enter into a cooperative arrangement for their mutual self-interest."[34]

31. Moo, *Epistle to the Romans*, 28 (emphasis in original). In the second edition of this commentary, Moo hedges these affirmations but still contends that the "'individual' question is at the center" (*Letter to the Romans*, 26).

32. Hauerwas, "Leaving Ruins," 38n14.

33. Hauerwas, "Church and Liberal Democracy," 81.

34. Hauerwas, 78. A commentator on Hauerwas's thought, Robert J. Dean, succinctly remarks on "the depersonalized politics of liberalism which envisions

For liberalism, this best occurs through two means. One is the means of the free market (to which I have paid more attention than does Hauerwas). Through the magical ministrations of Adam Smith's "invisible hand," the market amalgamates the various individual self-interests into the mutual self-interest of all. The desire—even greed—of individuals singly, blended in the free market, results in the greatest good for all.[35] If Christianity had formerly looked on limitless material acquisition with great suspicion, and always with a watchful eye to the welfare of the poor, liberalism said, "Let it be. Even if individuals enter the marketplace solely with their self-interest in mind, the market will combine and transform these interests so that as a whole, they will most effectively benefit all (or most)."

The second means, to which Hauerwas grants more attention, is that of proceduralism. Proceduralism says that we had best devise rules and policies that set morality and human ultimate ends, varied as they are, to one side. They are a private concern. In public, all will answer to rules and techniques that apply regardless of where they come from or what they embrace as their ultimate commitments. Has this worked? Hauerwas thinks not. Under liberalism,

---

self-sufficient individuals freed from the need to trust in or depend on anyone" (*For the Life*, 211).

35. After Smith, we have grabbed and retained only bits of his teaching, the invisible hand being the most famous. But Smith actually had a great deal to say about the importance of morality constraining and supplementing the market. Many historians argue that *The Wealth of Nations* should be interpreted in the light of Smith's earlier book, *Theory of Moral Sentiments*, which "can be read as a text in psychology or theology or ethics, or all of these" (Cox, *Market as God*, 158).

It was assumed that in making "morality" a matter of the "private sphere"—that is, what we do with our freedom—it could still be sustained and have an indirect public impact. But we know this has not been the case; our "private" morality has increasingly followed the form of our public life. People feel their only public duty is to follow their own interests as far as possible, limited only by the rule that we do not unfairly limit others' freedom. As a result we have found it increasingly necessary to substitute procedures and competition for the absence of public virtues. The bureaucracies in our lives are not simply the result of the complexities of industrialized society, but a requirement for a social order individualistically organized.[36]

This helps explain why the United States is such a litigious society. Absent thick customs and substantive communal bonds that direct us on how to treat one another and to watch out for the common good, we have resorted only to thin legal proceduralism: "Sue the bastard!" Bureaucracy also grows in the marketplace, where individuals have been trained to pursue their own maximal gain, and only more rules, forms, and minute oversight can curb their depredations. So we certainly can chafe at governmental regulations, but we actually lose more time navigating the maze of United Airlines' ticketing and reimbursement procedures, grappling with the labyrinthine intricacies of pharmaceutical and insurance bureaucracies, and trying to interpret the voluminous fine print bulking up our investment portfolios.[37]

36. Hauerwas, "Church and Liberal Democracy," 79.
37. On how modern bureaucracy owes at least as much to business, corporations, and the workings of the market as to the state and its regulations, see Graeber, *Utopia of Rules*, 10–13.

All told, says Hauerwas, "Liberalism becomes a self-fulfilling prophecy; a social order that is designed to work on the presumption that people are self-interested tends to produce that kind of people."[38] On the Christian account, sinful self-interest is strong enough without being anointed and isolated as the only effective human motivator. Liberalism has shorn us of higher commitments as social animals. It has concentrated on the individual and left individuals to their own devices to determine what they are free *for*—to what end or project they should devote their lives. In Hauerwas's pithy formulation, "We have made 'freedom of the individual' an end in itself and have ignored the fact that most of us do not have the slightest idea of what we should do with our freedom."[39]

Stripped of thick, substantive, particularistic, communal, ultimate commitments, in short, "we exist as individuals, but now 'individual' is but a name for a particular unit of arbitrary desires."[40] The individual as a unit of arbitrary desires means that I cannot look to you for aid in pursuits that we both might otherwise have regarded as goods. It means I need have no deep concern for you, or you for me. It means we guard most intensely a solely negative freedom, the freedom from one another's interference with the pursuit of our arbitrary, unshared desires. "The very genius of our society," says Hauerwas, "is to forge a political and social existence that does not have to depend on trusting others in matters important to our survival."[41]

In its atomistic individualism, in its disregard for the communal dimension of being human, in its concentration on negative

---

38. Hauerwas, "Church and Liberal Democracy," 79.
39. Hauerwas, 80.
40. Hauerwas, 81–82.
41. Hauerwas, 82.

freedom, "the story that liberalism teaches us is that we have no story, and as a result we fail to notice how deeply that story determines our lives."[42]

BOONS OF LIBERALISM AND CAPITALISM

I believe Hauerwas is right about liberalism as we now know it. But we do well to remember that liberalism has a history. It did not arise in a vacuum. And the seedbed in which it was born was Christianity. Despite its tendencies, it has borne and to a greatly diluted degree still bears the marks of its parentage. The philosopher Larry Siedentop summarizes, "The roots of liberalism were firmly established in the arguments of [Christian] philosophers and canon lawyers by the fourteenth and early fifteenth centuries: belief in a fundamental equality of status as the proper basis for a legal system; belief that enforcing moral conduct is a contradiction in terms; a defence of individual liberty, through the assertion or fundamental or 'natural' rights; and, finally, the conclusion that only a representative form of government is appropriate for a society resting on the assumption of moral equality [between individuals]."[43]

The church, following Scripture and tradition, saw all persons—however exalted or degraded their social status—as created in the image of God and redeemable by the work of Christ. David Bentley

---

42. Hauerwas, 84. Political philosopher Ronald Beiner makes a similar point: "Aristotle's most powerful insight is that in every society, moral life is based upon ethos, that is, character formation according to socially bred customs and habit. . . . Under the liberal dispensation, the ethos is—lack of ethos; individuals in this society are habituated to being insufficiently habituated" (*What's the Matter?*, 22).

43. Siedentop, *Inventing the Individual*, 332.

Hart notes that Christian teaching put charity, or graceful love, at its center, "as no pagan cult ever had, and raised the care of widows, orphans, the sick, the imprisoned, and the poor to the level of the highest of religious obligations."[44] After centuries of Christianity (which of course learned from its parent faith, Judaism), we take for granted the full and priceless personhood of every human being. But such valuation entered the ancient West "rather like a meteor from a clear sky. . . . For this reason, it is all but impossible for us to recover any real sense of the scandal that many pagans naturally felt at the bizarre prodigality with which the early Christians were willing to grant full humanity to persons of every class and condition, and of either sex."[45]

"Like a meteor from a clear sky," says Hart. The British theologian Oliver O'Donovan employs the same meteoric metaphor to indicate how Christianity marked and formed the West, including liberalism.[46] O'Donovan observes, "Like the surface of a planet pocked with craters by the bombardment it receives from space, the governments of the passing age show the impact of Christ's dawning glory."[47] O'Donovan adumbrates the signs of liberal society as aspirations to freedom, mercy in judgment, natural rights, and openness to the speech of everyone. All of these characteristics are based in Christianity. So, for instance, with free speech, "any voice within the public realm which could address the community about the common good had to be heard, lest the voice of true prophecy should go unheard."[48]

---

44. Hart, *Atheist Delusions*, 164.
45. Hart, 169.
46. Technically and more precisely a simile, I know. But allow me the alliteration.
47. O'Donovan, *Desire of the Nations*, 212.
48. O'Donovan, 252–71, quotation at 269.

Much as I like the meteoric metaphor, I want to invert the image. Imagine Jesus Christ's work—in his life, death, and resurrection—as a great shift in the tectonic plates underlying heaven and earth. From this shift arises a magnificent mountain, a mountain practically piercing the heavens and establishing a compass point reorienting all life on earth, with rivers flowing from it to water and nourish a parched, death-struck creation. Call it Mount Christ.

Now imagine liberalism as an entity and process partly and inevitably oriented by and grounding its foundations on Mount Christ. But liberalism over time obscures its origins. It "rests on the moral assumptions provided by Christianity." Yet it forgets the name of the mountain. It heedlessly strip-mines the mountaintop and spends its treasures prodigally. It blasts away much distinctive forestry, pulverizes landmark boulders, and reroutes some rivers. Put literally, "It preserves Christian ontology without the metaphysics of salvation."[49]

Doing so, liberalism impoverishes itself. Yet the mountain cannot be destroyed. Liberalism remains in its shadow, avails itself of the mountain's dwindled but still substantial treasure, lives by the now somewhat polluted water running off its back.[50] Thus liberalism has produced certain boons, gains genuinely valuable to humanity. These should be recognized and prized.

---

49. Siedentop, *Inventing the Individual*, 338.

50. Christianity, and the civic republicanism also at the root of America's founding, casts a shadow too in slowing the acidic effects of atomizing individualism. The Pilgrims and later Puritans who came ashore here ventured not as solitary individuals but as men, women, and children in communities—as churches. Thus their individualism, if it was that, was an *embedded* individualism, nested in the context of communities. For an account mindful of communal strains in the American founding, see the political scientist Barry Alan Shain's *The Myth of American Individualism*.

One boon of liberalism is the proclaimed equality of all persons. Liberalism has proceeded to a partial, sometimes halting but still significant embrace of this equality. In the liberal tradition, the Declaration of Independence insists that all persons are created equal. It holds this truth to be "self-evident." In fact, it is not self-evident to everyone, everywhere, and at all times. It is not apparent, for instance, to the atheist evolutionist that people are created; they appear instead to be the result of a haphazard but complexifying process unfolding over eons. Nor is it apparent to, say, the white supremacist that all people are equally made and valued as bearers of the image of the God who creates them. That all persons are created equal is a product of revelation, Jewish and Christian.[51]

Still, liberalism as it has historically developed has held to the truth of human equality, however suspended in air that affirmation may be once it is hoisted off its revelational foundations. In its revelational basis, human equality stands on the Trinitarian Father, Son, and Holy Spirit. The Father created all in his image. The Son bestowed salvation on all, of whatever gender, ethnicity, or social status. The Spirit at Pentecost poured gifts of grace on men and women of all tongues and nations. Thus liberalism, even removed from its revelational basis, has at least ideally held up the equality of all before and under the law, not favoring the rich over the poor. It has steadily extended voting and property-holding rights to men of all races, and finally to women. It has abolished racially separate and (actually) unequal drinking fountains, restaurants, hotel accommodations, schools, and so forth. It has granted equal dignity to the disabled or differently abled. Holding to the truth of the equality of

---

51. For a remarkable account of the Christian particularity of human equality and human rights spanning Christian (and concomitantly Western) history, see Holland, *Dominion*.

all, liberalism has more recently paid attention to sexual orientation and identity. At its best, it has insisted that *all*, no matter how small their sexual minority, should have rights and privileges equal to any majority.

A second boon of liberalism is its quest for peace. This too has a revelational basis. Jesus went to his death on the cross without violently avenging his enemies. And his early followers took up the cross in the same way, disavowing vengeance on their enemies.[52] This is not to say that liberalism has always been peaceful—far from it. But it originated in a tumultuous world, torn by the seemingly constant violent strife of the conflicts between religious groups and incipient nation-states. The early liberal Thomas Hobbes, sometimes living in exile for fear of his safety, strived to arrive at a means to get people to live together without killing each other. Hobbes's answer is not one we later moderns can entirely endorse: he believed that ultimately, the mutual fear of a leviathan, a state sovereign with power beyond contestation, would quell the violence of all against all. But even if we do not accept Hobbes's solution, we may appreciate his questing—and that of subsequent liberals—for a peaceful, nonviolent common life.[53]

Yet a third boon of liberalism is its suspicion of coercion. The revelational basis here rests on creation by a loving triune God who created all that is out of sheer love and delight. Such a God, incarnate in Christ, offers grace and wholeness to all, even as the loving Spirit sustains life and goodness in all that exists. Ultimately, what God wants from God's creation is not enforced compliance but responsive and uncoerced love. Again, liberalism

52. For elaboration on this point of the cross and nonviolence, see my *New Creation*, 46–52.

53. On Hobbes and his yearning for peace, see Davies, *Nervous States*, 33–36.

forgets and attenuates the revelational basis but in its own way attempts to minimize coercion—hence, for example, representational government.

In instancing such boons of liberalism and noting their Christian origins, I do not mean to imply that Christianity or the church has nothing to learn from liberalism. Mount Christ arose suddenly, earthshakingly, and apocalyptically, and its full meaning and ramifications take centuries to absorb.[54] The church, and not just the world, has often been slow on the uptake. Far from perfect, the church has grievously and repeatedly failed. Sometimes it has been liberalism that has nudged the church toward a better version of itself. On matters such as equal standing, peace, and noncoercion, it has forced the church back to a reimmersion in the wellspring on the top of Mount Christ, preeminently to the Scriptures and the story of Israel and Jesus. It has, for example, indirectly reminded Christians that "God does not want the church to evangelize the world through the coercive apparatus of civil authority, for to do so is to try to wrest control of history from God's hands."[55]

What about capitalism, liberalism's twin? May we also speak of its boons? It would be dishonest and churlish to deny the amazing productive capacities of capitalism. Surely it has played a role in lifting masses of people out of poverty and into a way of life that includes comforts formerly, if ever, enjoyed only by royalty. Capitalism can be a tremendous prod to creativity. And despite its

---

54. I have in mind here such phenomena as the eventual abolition of (legal) slavery and the nonsubordination of women. It has taken centuries in these cases to break off from "the futile ways inherited from your ancestors" (1 Pet 1:18), but the church has responded to the gospel as if to a time bomb on a delayed setting. See the masterful discussion of deSilva, *Honor, Patronage*, 233–39.

55. Cavanaugh, *Field Hospital*, 166; see also 168 and 233.

destructiveness, it does not approach that of state-directed communisms in the USSR and China, which were directly and indirectly responsible for the deaths of millions. Give capitalism its real-world due.

At the same time, we have been prone to credit capitalism for boons not exclusive to it. For instance, the increase in the human life span is often credited to capitalism. Yet here we have more primarily to thank clean water and antibiotics—goods not invented solely or even especially by capitalism. Anthropologist David Graeber cannily observes that gains in productivity, hygiene, education, and science are often blankly attributed to capitalism. But, he contends, "it is . . . by no means clear to me that all these improvements can be attributed to a single entity called 'capitalism'—or whether it is more sensible to see capitalist economic advances, advances in scientific knowledge, and democratic politics as essentially independent phenomena, any one of which can occur in the absence of either of the others."[56]

LIBERALISM TODAY

To avert confusion, it may be helpful at this juncture to make clear that the "liberalism" I have been discussing is not simply that political configuration regularly attacked on Fox News, abjured by the Tucker Carlsons and Sean Hannitys as the fixation of "libtards." Liberalism in fact is much older than the divide between the currently styled "conservatives" and "liberals." It encompasses both.

For nineteenth-century liberals, now best considered as classical liberals, the motor and foundation for the construction of

---

56. Graeber, *Debt*, 355.

a free society was the free-market economy.[57] Classical liberalism dominated in the United States from the end of the Civil War until the Great Depression. It was severely shaken by World War I and by the end of World War II was "almost completely discredited."[58] Extreme concentrations of power and wealth in the capitalist class were perceived as gross and unacceptable. The Great Depression was a collapse of the system, marking the first time within a century when government would save capitalism from itself. (The second time came with government bailouts following the crash of 2008.)

Franklin Delano Roosevelt's herculean efforts, with the work programs and Keynesian economic policies of the New Deal, averted total disaster. FDR's presidency, from 1933 to 1945, initiated what might best be called reform liberalism. While classical liberals fear government as the greatest threat to individual freedom, reform liberals worry at least equally about the instability of capitalism and exaggerated concentrations of corporate business power. Early on, the New Deal was enthusiastically supported by the working class, lower middle classes, and farmers, all of whom were burdened by untrammeled capitalism.

But if classical liberalism had been almost completely discredited, it never entirely went away. Champions of the unleashed free market went into a kind of hibernation—less in the public eye and certainly less at the reins but still thinking and planning a reemergence. Incidentally, many evangelicals never welcomed or entirely embraced the New Deal and the "big government" it entailed. As reform liberalism developed decades after FDR's death,

---

57. For the following discussion of classical and reform liberalism, I rely on Jardine, *Making and Unmaking*, 33–77.
58. Jardine, 67.

the evangelicals would find the opportunity to ally with (other) free-market liberals, including those who cared more about the free market itself than any religious concerns.

To conceive and implement his New Deal policies, FDR turned to experts in economics, science, sociology, and engineering. Thus reform liberalism was marked by the cult of the scientific manager. Most such managers favored secular expertise. Although not necessarily averse to faith communities, they believed the public world was best operated on secular, supposedly universal terms. After the postwar period, "reform liberals attempted to create a more thoroughly secular, and therefore, in their eyes, more neutral [and scientific] system."[59] By the 1960s and 1970s, this entailed sloughing off many laws that had a considerable cultural basis in Christian morality. So no-fault divorce was instituted, blue laws guarding Sabbatarian observances and curtailing alcoholic consumption collapsed, abortion was legalized, the censorship of entertainment ended, and restrictions on gambling were reduced.

This set the stage for the so-called culture wars. Evangelical Christianity (of a broad sort, including both conservative and more comparatively liberal kinds) had been politically and socially dominant in the United States in the nineteenth century. Now as the twentieth century drew nearer to its close, the Christian sway over the entire social and cultural landscape was diminishing. "Secular humanism" was one of the targets easiest to blame.

White conservative evangelicals—then self-styled as "fundamentalists"—were shocked, in addition, by government moves to withdraw tax exemptions for racially segregated schools. This only raised their ire against "big government" and secularism.

59. Jardine, 77.

Meanwhile, on the political right, operatives sensed that much of the old New Deal confederation, including many evangelically oriented rural and southern Americans, was frayed and divided. The operatives saw that the race issue aggravated a growing evangelical animus against reform liberalism and cast about for a more amenable and respectable way to draw evangelicals into their fold. Antiabortionism (happily also attractive to Roman Catholics increasingly disenchanted with reform liberalism) fit the bill. It politically activated evangelicals, even as their theological concentration on individualism continued.[60]

In the backlash from free market champions and (predominantly white) evangelicals and other culture warriors, reform liberalism lost its dominance by 1980 with the first election of Ronald Reagan. Reform liberalism, like classical liberalism before it, remains alive but no longer regnant. Classical liberalism, meanwhile, still has its champions but in its most significant current form has morphed into neoliberalism, to which we now turn.

60. For more detail on this history, see Balmer, *Thy Kingdom Come*.

2

THE SPECIAL CASE OF NEOLIBERALISM

Liberalism has undergone various transmutations over the course of its history. With the shift from classical to reform liberalism through the middle of the twentieth century, it chastened the market and, to a degree, empowered government and civil society. But there were those who never accepted this sea change. Since the 1980s, they have successfully rolled back the tide and asserted power. The liberal regime under which we now live and labor is neoliberalism.

Neoliberalism does not see the market as a facet of society, as embedded within and subordinated to the moral and spiritual aims of a people. Rather, for neoliberalism, the market encompasses and defines the entirety of society.[1] Liberalism posited a division of the public (government) and the private (civil society, the economy,

---

1. See Ryan LaMothe's ten features of the neoliberal social imaginary, all centered on and under the market (*Care of Souls*, 169–70). See also Philip Mirowski's "thirteen commandments of neoliberalism" (*Never Let a Serious Crisis*, 53–67). See too the nuanced overview by Kevin Hargaden, *Theological Ethics*, 1–33. Finally, see the incisive summary by Matthew Eggemeier, *Against Empire*, 15–27.

the family). But the line between the public and the private could and did blur; this smudged line was thus the locus of most political battles through the twentieth century. So classical liberals criticized the New Deal's expansion of public or state action into previously "private" citadels of economic power and civil society as an illegitimate incursion—then labeled it "liberal." Later, the civil rights movement toiled to extend racial equality to "private" civil institutions and employments or businesses such as restaurants, hotels, trains, and buses. Again, many classical liberals recoiled, denouncing the proposed changes as "liberal" overreach and invasion. But the accusations of trespassing the supposedly sacrosanct public-private borderline could fly both ways. It was reform liberals who squawked when classical liberals, characterized as "conservatives," wanted public laws criminalizing miscegenation, abortion and birth control, "sodomy," and pornography. Consequently, there has raged a constant struggle or vexed negotiation—a decidedly political struggle and negotiation—over what is "private" and what is "public" and the seemly privileges of each.[2]

The face and substance of politics change under neoliberalism. Neoliberalism is a panoply of cultural and political-economic practices that sets marketized competition at the center of social life—even as the sole ruler of social life. It aims to create a society that does not merely include markets but is based on the market and where there are, right down to the dirt under the fingernails of

2. See Duggan, *Twilight of Equality?*, 7–8. In this regard, political philosopher Seyla Benhabib makes the following (perhaps too sweeping) claim: "All struggles against oppression in the modern world begin by redefining what had previously been considered 'private,' non-public and non-political issues as matters of public concern, as issues of justice, as sites of power which need discursive legitimation" (cited in Horrell, *Solidarity and Difference*, 78).

flesh-and-blood individuals, only agonizing private enterprises. "In neoliberal society, the capitalist market is no longer imagined as a distinct arena where goods are valued and exchanged; rather, the market is, or ideally should be, the basis for *all* of society."[3] Politics is no longer primarily a negotiation of where the line between public and private falls, for neoliberalism "works to erase this line between public and private and to create an entire society—in fact, an entire world—based on private, market competition. . . . Consequently, contemporary politics take shape around questions of how best to promote competition."[4]

If an earlier liberalism imagined people as fundamentally and finally individuals, freed of the need for or interference from other individuals, neoliberalism sees people as individuals existing at the behest of the market, pitted in competition against one another. Thus liberalism

> morphed into the neoliberal Market Everlasting: unfettered free trade and globalization, epitomized by the formation of the World Trade Organization in 1995; the privatization of public services and their lucrative relegation to the caprice of the marketplace; the "reinvention" of government agencies along the line of corporate bureaucracies; and the maniacal deregulation of finance and industry under the rubric of "modernization," liberating corporations from "stifling" restrictions on their freedom to invest, pollute, and exploit. Under the aegis of the World Trade Organization, the World Bank, and the International Monetary Fund, globalization built a paradise of capital, with its incandescent minarets

3. Wilson, *Neoliberalism*, 2–3.
4. Wilson, 23.

ascending on every continent, looming over multitudes pauperized into despair, impressed into the legions of wage servitude, or sedated by the opiates of the spectacle.[5]

All political configurations serve certain interests. Neoliberalism serves the interests of private property owners, businesses, multinational corporations, and financiers.[6] And it does so avidly and, on occasion, fiercely. Naturalized and considered the epitome or end of history, it resembles nothing "so much as a caricature of Marxist historical determinism. It merely substitute[s] liberal capitalism for communism in claiming that here we [behold] the final form of human society."[7] So neoliberalism can be characterized not sensationally but soberly as "the Marxism of the ruling classes."[8]

NEOLIBERALISM'S DEVELOPMENT

From its early days to the midcareer of its development, neoliberalism was generally regarded as radical and even dangerous. Through much of the twentieth century, Keynesianism ruled, checking the vagaries and excesses of capitalism. But some European and American theorists chafed at Keynesianism and any restriction of the market. The Walter Lippmann Colloquium, gathered in 1938, included many of these thinkers. More significantly, Friedrich von Hayek convened like-minded thinkers at Mont Pelerin (Switzerland) in 1947. The Mont Pelerin Society decisively sowed the seeds of what has now ripened into full-blown neoliberalism.

5. McCarraher, *Enchantments of Mammon*, 663.
6. Harvey, *Brief History of Neoliberalism*, 7.
7. B. Kunkel, quoted in Rogers-Vaughn, *Caring for Souls*, 233.
8. Steve Fraser, *Age of Acquiescence*, 416.

Society members like Ludwig von Mises argued that only the market, not economic planning, was efficient and capable of calculating the value of goods in real time. They conceived of the market not so much as an ultimately benevolent invisible hand as a vast information processor. Eschewing any human or rational control of the market, they also denied a place for considering ultimate human ends or purposes. "What are humans for?" was a question cast aside, to be ignored as irrelevant. Mises argued first and foremost for the technical and scientific efficiency of the market and not at all for its morality. In fact, Mises was a moral relativist who believed "there was no objective way of gauging the right amount of goods to [be] produced"[9] or even what were true and higher human goods to be served by market commodities.[10] For Mises, as the political economist William Davies puts it, "A planned economy required experts to establish facts on questions that were really all a matter of personal perspective. Markets, on the other hand, save us from all having to agree on what is needed."[11] In other words, neoliberals propose a market utopia in which politics—the negotiation of jostling human goods and striving for the common good—is obsolete.

Hayek was dubious of consensus on any moral or political subject, believing that consensus flirted with socialism. Accordingly, he did not like trying to establish generally agreed-upon facts and was suspicious of any "experts" who might do so. Thus for Mises and

9. Quoted in Davies, *Nervous States*, 155.

10. For suggestive theological leads on recovering the quest for truth in this post-truth milieu, see Long, *Truth Telling*. For an incisive critique of neoliberal agnotology—the science of ignorance—and its obscurantist application to climate change and the link between cigarettes and lung cancer, see Mirowski, *Never Let a Serious Crisis*, 226–30.

11. Davies, *Nervous States*, 155.

Hayek, the market serves as a kind of "post-truth" institution. It "saves us from having to know what is going on overall" and indeed works "*better* if we ignore the facts of the system at large, and focus only on the part of it that concerns us."[12] As a gigantic information processor, the market acts as a "mass sensory device . . . that exists to detect sentiment and changes in public mood." And "understood as real-time monitoring devices, markets are not so much tools for producing facts but for gauging our feelings. This is where faith in the market maps onto populism and nationalism, for all these creeds see politics as little other than mass coordination via shared feeling."[13]

Emphasizing ignorance, uncertainty, and the maelstrom of fleeting moods and emotions, the Austrian neoliberals saw individuals thrust into competition within the vortex of the market, the gargantuan information processor that would determine winners in an otherwise incomprehensible contest. Mises idealized the entrepreneur because the entrepreneur was brave (or reckless?) enough to risk all, to plunge into the market contest, unclear of the outcome, of what techniques would work, or of what commodities would sell. This bravery reminded Mises of nothing so much as soldiers rushing into the fog of war—threatened, unassured of success, beset by insecurity but *acting*. This "courageous and strategic mind-set" was similar "to the qualities that [the Prussian military theorist] Carl von Clausewitz had applauded in great generals."[14] Accordingly, "Austrian economics [with the likes of Mises and later Joseph Schumpeter] . . . sought to channel the aristocratic, military ethos into the realm of entrepreneurial combat."[15] Henceforth,

12. Davies, 167.
13. Davies, 167.
14. Davies, 156.
15. Davies, 157.

neoliberalism would apotheosize the entrepreneur as the model, or quintessential, human.

The New Right was drawn to neoliberal ideas and spread them through think tanks derived from the Mont Pelerin Society, including the Heritage Foundation, the World Economic Forum, and the Center for Policy Studies. Liberals of various stripes were attracted by neoliberalism's enshrinement of freedom, which they saw as topping all other virtues. Committed liberals found neoliberalism's freedom—decidedly a negative freedom, trumpeting noninterference by other individuals—almost irresistible. As geographer David Harvey observes, "Any political movement that holds individual freedoms to be sacrosanct is vulnerable to incorporation into the neoliberal fold."[16] But note again that neoliberalism's version of freedom is negative freedom: freedom *from* with no corresponding notion of what freedom is *for*. The economic historian Philip Mirowski writes that the "peculiar brand of [neoliberal] freedom is not the realization of any political, human, or cultural telos, but rather the positing of autonomous self-governed entities, all coming naturally equipped with some version of 'rationality' and motives of ineffable self-interest, striving to improve their lot in life by engaging in market exchange." In this framework, "everyone is treated as expressing untethered context-free hankering, as if they were born yesterday into solitary confinement; this is the hidden heritage of the entrepreneurialism of the self."[17]

Emphasizing a rendition of freedom that most liberals were unequipped to resist, neoliberal ideas spread and took root in the

---

16. Harvey, *Brief History of Neoliberalism*, 41. In the penultimate sentence of his book, Harvey declares, "There is a far, far nobler prospect of freedom to be won than that which neoliberalism preaches" (206).

17. Mirowski, *Never Let a Serious Crisis*, 61.

halls of power. Ideas that were previously regarded as radical and dangerous entered the intellectual mainstream, exemplified by the Nobel Prize in economics being awarded to Hayek in 1974 and to Milton Friedman in 1976. The first opportunity to put neoliberalism into practice on a statewide scale occurred in Chile. The leader of a military junta that, backed by the United States, seized power in 1973, General Augusto Pinochet relied on the counsel of University of Chicago–trained neoliberals in an effort to remold his country. As it happened, the experiment failed economically during the Latin American debt crisis of 1982. But Pinochet brutally ruled as a dictator until 1990, kidnapping, torturing, and killing resisters.[18] Shying away from association with Pinochet's infamous cruelty, neoliberals subsequently tended to eschew the term *neoliberalism* to name their position.[19] It was shrewder and strategically preferable to go generally unnamed, emphasizing instead the asserted ineluctability and naturalness and freedom of the market and the wisdom of subordinating all of society to it.

Named or unnamed, neoliberalism ascended with the elections of Margaret Thatcher and Ronald Reagan, in 1979 and 1980, respectively. Thatcher and Reagan extolled the market, busted unions, and attacked the welfare state. In *The Road to Serfdom*, Hayek had written, "This is really the crux of the matter. Economic control is not merely control of a sector of human life which can

18. For an excellent journalistic account of Pinochet's Chile and neoliberal participation, see Klein, *Shock Doctrine*. For a brilliant theological engagement, see Cavanaugh, *Torture and Eucharist*.

19. Actually, chroniclers disagree on when neoliberals became averse to the label. Mirowski observes, "The people associated with the doctrine *did* call themselves 'neo-liberals' . . . from the 1930s to the early 1950s, but then they abruptly stopped the practice" (*Never Let a Serious Crisis*, 38). Certainly the term grew less appealing to proponents after Pinochet.

be separated from the rest; it is the control of the means for all our ends." Similarly, Thatcher in 1981 said, "Economics are the method; the object is to change the heart and soul." Thatcher's anthropology, like the neoliberals', was resolutely individualistic. As she famously remarked, "There is no such thing as society; only individual men and women, and families."[20] (It is hard to see how the same reasoning could not be applied to deny the reality of the market.)

Meanwhile, Reagan proclaimed in his first inaugural address, "In this present crisis, government is not the solution to our problem: government is the problem."[21] Knocking government's supposed ineffectiveness, Reagan began a move toward privatizing institutions and practices that had formerly been government-owned or managed. Education, health care, and even prison ownership and operation would be increasingly shoved into the private sector, and the government itself was reshaped in mimicry (and service) of the corporation. Reagan privatized everything from airlines to telecommunications to finance. Meanwhile, he reduced the top marginal tax rate from 70 to 28 percent in what was billed as the "largest tax cut in history."[22]

If the American move to neoliberalism was initiated by Republicans, its development and maturation were bipartisan. Democratic President Bill Clinton practically eliminated welfare as it had existed for the prior sixty years with his "welfare reform" bill of 1996, leaving more avid postage stamp collectors in the United States than welfare recipients.[23] Clinton also devised and

20. Quotes in this paragraph are from Rogers-Vaughn, *Caring for Souls*, 42 and 70.
21. Wilson, *Neoliberalism*, 37.
22. Harvey, *Brief History of Neoliberalism*, 26.
23. Rogers-Vaughn, *Caring for Souls*, 117.

instituted the North American Free Trade Agreement (1994), releasing capital to move more freely across national borders. In addition, he signed into law the repeal of the Glass-Steagall Act, which had existed since 1933 and had served to enforce the separation of commercial banking and speculative investment so that banks couldn't gamble with customers' savings.[24] Subsequently, "the 'financial economy' has grown so massively that the value of financial assets now exceeds the global output of all goods and services—the part that is called the 'real economy'—by a factor of ten. This expansion has resulted in what some call an 'inverted' or a 'casino' economy."[25] Overall, Clinton was so bullish about the ascendancy of neoliberalism that he resorted to biblical, apocalyptic language to hail its worldwide spread as ushering in "the fullness of time" (see Gal 4:4 and Eph 1:10).[26]

Neoliberalism continues unabated to the present. It featured in Obama's governing, which was in part a call for justice and equality, but not as ends in themselves. Rather, he pitched this call as "a means to achieve the neoliberal end of economic growth and competitiveness."[27] And it has been exemplified in Trump's tax cuts (markedly favoring the already wealthy), his dismissal of the poor as negligible "losers," and his divisive, bullying rhetoric. In a society engulfed by market competition, the "discourse of the common good and compassion withers," and "the only vocabulary left is that

---

24. Rogers-Vaughn cites Saskia Sassen: "While traditional banking is about selling money that the bank has, finance is about selling something it does not have" (111). Finance focuses on the buying and selling of what "the bank does not have." What "the bank does not have" is unpaid debt.

25. Cox, *Market as God*, 102.

26. McCarraher, *Enchantments of Mammon*, 665.

27. Eggemeier and Fritz, *Send Lazarus*, 79. See also Wilson, *Neoliberalism*, 89–90.

of the bully—one that takes pride in the civic-enervating binary of winners and losers."[28]

INEQUALITY: BACK TO ROMAN LEVELS

Market competition now pervades our lives. Indeed, it defines our very selves. And the competition does not occur on an even playing field. Crowning market competition, neoliberalism actively downplays and hobbles democracy, for democracy would have the many rebelling against arrangements favoring only the few "winners." For its establishment, neoliberalism has relied on executive and judicial decisions rather than democratic legislation. Relatedly, it has relied "on undemocratic and unaccountable institutions (such as the Federal Reserve or the IMF) to make key decisions. This creates the paradox [or the outright contradiction] of intense state interventions and government by elites and 'experts' in a world where the state is not supposed to be interventionist."[29]

Neoliberalism renders competition normative and legitimate in every sphere of life. And the necessary outcome of unrelenting competition is inequality. Not surprisingly, wealth now concentrates at the tip-top of the American economic pyramid. Between 1978 and 2015, the uppermost 10 percent of earners realized a 115 percent increase in their income, while the top 0.001 percent enjoyed a stupendous rise of 685 percent. By 2018, half of the

---

28. Henry Giroux, cited in Wilson, *Neoliberalism*, 208. Eggemeier and Fritz comment, "The election of a businessman with no political experience and little knowledge of the Constitution, democratic norms and procedures, or judicial principles reveals the extent to which neoliberalism has been successful at capturing the political sense of citizens and recasting the function of the state in economic terms" (*Send Lazarus*, 80).
29. Harvey, *Brief History of Neoliberalism*, 6.

world's wealth rested in hands of just forty-two persons. Amazon's Jeff Bezos makes many times more every minute than the average American makes in a year.[30]

Dwell for a moment on the take-home of American CEOs compared to that of rank-and-file employees. In 2018, the average chief executive of an S&P 500 company earned 287 times more than their median employee. Elon Musk made 40,668 times more money than the median Tesla employee. But we need not focus on the extreme of the extremes. Since so many employees are found in retail and food service, we might consider the pay ratios of executives to that of their median worker of Gap clothing (3,566 to 1) or McDonald's (2,124 to 1). Does a Gap executive, however brilliant or hardworking, really do 3,566 times the work of a median-level employee? What wonders must the McDonald's CEO work to genuinely earn (i.e., deserve) 2,124 times his frontline cooks and cashiers? And has the CEOs' reasonable value actually increased nearly tenfold since 1970, when the median ratio of executive compensation was 30 to 1?[31]

On the uneven neoliberal playing field, the economy as a whole may grow while many or most suffer economic stagnation or decline. And that is exactly what has happened. Half the American population has seen no economic progress for nearly forty years.[32] Unemployment statistics do not include the underemployed, who find work that is hardly satisfying, low paying, and often comes without benefits or job security. They do not include those who work two or more jobs to survive. Meanwhile, the cost of living rises, housing

30. Davies, *Nervous States*, 76–77, 173.
31. Statistics in this paragraph are from Campbell, "CEOs Made 287 Times"; and Harvey, *Brief History of Neoliberalism*, 16.
32. Davies, *Nervous States*, 77.

costs soar out of control, and increased debt is assumed. While the stock market booms, total income balloons, unemployment falls, and "winners" receive extreme rewards, vast swathes of the populace are financially underwater or gasping with it up to their noses.

Overall, what we can now boast of is an economy that in its inequality compares to that of ancient Rome. It has been estimated that the top four hundred taxpayers in the United States exercise ten thousand times the material power of the average citizen in the bottom 90 percent. This differs little from the gap between Roman senators and the slaves and farm laborers who comprised most of the population.[33]

Excessive inequality erodes democracy and strains to bursting the social fabric. It raises stressful questions about injustice and does violence to any notion of shared citizenship. It batters all sense of common belonging or that there might be any such thing as a common good. The competitiveness of the marketplace, unchecked, pits Americans against Americans and goes a long way toward explaining why the country is now so divided and riven. Unfortunately, division and hostility are often misidentified or misdirected against immigrants or those of other races. What goes unnamed is the neoliberal framework that entraps us all.

THE ENTREPRENEURIAL SELF

"Economics are the method; the object is to change the heart and soul," said Margaret Thatcher. What Thatcher hoped for has come to pass. Neoliberalism has transformed us—heart, body, and soul. Suffusing our identities and the relationships that constitute them, the market swallows us whole.

---

33. Block and Somers, *Power of Market Fundamentalism*, 3.

If humans were *homo sapiens*, the wise species, we are now *homo economicus*, the economic and economizing species. Reshaped and trained, habituated to consider ourselves solely in light of economic and contractual relations, we now consider the entrepreneur the ideal and model human being.

The problem is not entrepreneurialism as a role or occasional practice. The problem is that under neoliberal capitalism, we are relentlessly coached and shaped to see ourselves as nothing but entrepreneurs. Our bodies, our talents, our relationships, our education, our training are put into all-consuming service to market competition, with the objective becoming "an ever-increasing gross domestic product in one's person."[34]

No aspect of our lives escapes the neoliberal reconceptualization of the essential self as entrepreneur. At leisure as well as at work, we must constantly consider how we may most profitably present ourselves. My presence on and contributions to social media, no less than my résumé, become fodder for the capitalization and enhancement of my image or personal "brand." I post photos of my home and interior design to express and advantage my entrepreneurial self. Likewise with snaps of my travels and standout, representative meals. I build a self by my association (and selfies, glory be!) with artists, musicians, and celebrities. Considered entrepreneurially, shopping becomes neoliberal labor, where I carefully construct and display the self with representative clothing, electronic devices, and other symbolic commodities—the self that I exploit to self-appreciate, to grow my brand, to increase my personal gross domestic product.[35] In short, I am a hustler, always hustling.

---

34. Tanner, *Christianity and the New Spirit*, 73.
35. See Wilson, *Neoliberalism*, 136.

Notice, too, how neoliberal capitalistic competition so thoroughly enlists the body. Botox, plastic surgery and body sculpturing, and dental implants are means of transforming the body to present a maximally attractive, youthful, and energetic self. Only such a self is fitted to perform in and react to the ever-demanding, fast-changing market. The self, very much including the body, gets fragmented into a "jumble of assets to be invested, nurtured, managed, and developed; but equally an offsetting inventory of liabilities to be pruned, outsourced, shorted, hedged against, and minimized."[36]

If fragmentation of the self is one aspect of neoliberal anthropology, flexibility is another. Itself global and emphatically not tied to any one place, the market encourages radical individualism, with loose or nonexisting bonds to particular traditions and locations. The disencumbered individual must be ever ready to move and otherwise change to meet shifting job and market demands. As Mirowski comments, "The *summum bonum* of modern agency is to present oneself as eminently *flexible* in any and all respects."[37]

Clearly much is demanded and expected of the neoliberal individual. But that individual is guaranteed or promised nothing in return for a complete submission to market competition. Corporations may lay off workers at will. Individuals may suffer accidents and catastrophes. But in all events, they can be cast off and driven back to their own individualized resources. Wendy Brown remarks, "As [purely] human capital, the [neoliberal] subject is at once in charge of itself, responsible for itself, and yet a potential disposable element of the whole."[38] Desperate enough, the disposable individual may always sell blood plasma, enroll in a drug trial, rent out

36. Mirowski, *Never Let a Serious Crisis*, 108.
37. Mirowski, 108.
38. Quoted in LaMothe, *Care of Souls*, 176.

her body as a surrogate mother, or even resort to some discreet prostitution. Whatever. The market does not care or have room for care.

The neoliberal mantra of "personal responsibility" must be seen in this light. Individuals are constantly exhorted to assume personal responsibility; however, "neoliberalism's promotion of a culture of personal responsibility is harsh and unrealistic. It suggests that, regardless of situation or circumstance, we, as individuals, should be fully responsible for what happens to us, even those things that are out of our control. . . . If something bad happens, look inward, not outward, for answers or redress." Accordingly, it elides histories and political and economic structures like racism, capitalism, and patriarchy. Thus "while personal responsibility might seem like a neutral, uncontroversial cultural value, in the context of neoliberalism, it becomes a vehicle of intensified oppression that renders this intensified oppression invisible and even impossible to articulate."[39]

Emphasizing ceaseless competition, insisting on obsession with image and self-presentation, pervading work and "free time" alike, completely co-opting and managing the body, fragmenting the self and bending it to maximal adaptability and flexibility, neoliberal capitalism "reduces human beings to an arbitrary bundle of 'investments,' skill sets, temporary alliances (family, sex, race), and fungible body parts."[40] Professional actors are virtuosos of physical comportment, mastering their bodies like sophisticated instruments employed to communicate through bearing, gesture, facial expression, and verbal intonation. Ever "on" in the competitive theater of neoliberalism, we are all to some significant degree actors in our own lives, moving from role to role and consumed by each successive character.

39. Both quotes in this paragraph are from Wilson, *Neoliberalism*, 61.
40. Mirowski, *Never Let a Serious Crisis*, 59.

More darkly, this acting easily blurs into con artistry. For example, service workers are coached and trained to cunningly deploy their own pleasant affect to maximize sales (and tips). Any "real" feeling that remains is often distant and diluted. In on the game as we all are, we become suspicious of those treating us with respect and affection; they may only be conducting a scam, we may only or mainly be objects of manipulation and exploitation. So the already frayed social fabric suffers further tears.

More darkly yet, when entrepreneurialism becomes the essence (such as it is) of the self and is always in the service of selling itself, we come perilously close to something that may most honestly—and realistically—be called prostitution. What, after all, is prostitution except the successful presentation of an attractive body for sale? And what is the entrepreneurial self if not body and soul totally enlisted in an unending hustle, the next sale?[41]

The best art always reflects, and reflects on, its times. As neoliberal capitalism has unfolded, art has engaged it.[42] But few works have more outstandingly or revelatorily captured our current milieu than the 2019 film *Uncut Gems*. It centers on the jewel dealer and gambler Howard Ratner—a rat in an unending race. The film opens with images of a valuable opal, the gem fading into a galaxy of stars and planets. Right away we are told that this is a depiction of our world, our universe. We then move to Ratner undergoing a colonoscopy, the camera invading his body and revealing in his entrails another glistening universe; thus the gem's galaxy and Howard's body are connected. Immediately we cut to Ratner on the street, yelling into his cell phone, and the film's pace will not

41. True to their creed, neoliberals such as Milton Friedman favor the legalization of prostitution. See Ammeson, "Interview with Milton Friedman."
42. For a salutary such novel, see Mountford, *Young Man's Guide.*

relent for the remainder of its two-hour running time. Ratner constantly cuts deals—sometimes two at a time—frenetically converses on his cell and with interlocutors literally in his face (and sometimes both at once), fronts his precious opals, seeks to impress an NBA athlete and other customers, fends off the loan sharks who shadow him, and places high-stakes bets on basketball games. Howard is the consummate hustler, and his hustle is on from sunup to bedtime. Like a careening juggler, he must keep all the balls in the air; if one falls, they all do. But of course, eventually, one ball will fall. So the film ends tragically, and the camera zooms in on a gunshot wound, then again enters the body, this time into Howard's veins and bloodstream. We have come full circle. We have entered his universe, body and soul, and his has interpenetrated ours. Under neoliberalism, we are all, if not quite as desperately as Howard Ratner, hustlers—ceaselessly bent on self-capitalization, on leveraging one deal into a bigger one, too often only one step from disaster. For neoliberal capitalism, we are nothing but uncut gems, vendable body-and-soul resources in the competitive marketplace. "We do not simply access the means of production; we have *become* the means of production."[43]

The film grinds you down. When I saw it at the theater, I went with two companions. One walked out. The other saw it through to the end, then admitted to exhaustion and stomach sickness. But that, I think, is exactly the point. Does neoliberalism leave us with any real or desirable way to live, to be a self?[44]

---

43. Rogers-Vaughn, *Caring for Souls*, 152.

44. Yet another movie scrutinizing the age of neoliberalism is *Hustlers* (2019). At its conclusion, the stripper–hustler–con artist Ramona observes, "This whole country is a strip club. You got people tossing the money and people doing the dance."

THE STATE OF PRECARITY

Noticing the tenuous, fragile, breathless, edge-of-the cliff quality of life under present-day capitalism, some astute observers of neoliberalism, playing on the term *precarious*, have begun to speak of our state as one of "precarity." Given vertiginous scales of inequality and the redefinition of the self as entrepreneurial, we are thrust on an uneven playing field into a crisis of competition without respite. Many among us are "losers" in this constant contest.

And what to do with the "losers"? They are deemed disposables (and remember, we are all ultimately disposable under neoliberalism). And so we see poor folk—especially poor folk of color—killed by police without consequence. We see postindustrial communities no longer deemed valuable by state governments and left without clean, safe drinking water, as in Flint, Michigan. We see poor youth abandoned without affordable and excellent education. We see refugees forced to flee their homes by war or social and economic collapse but rejected at the border or forced to languish in refugee camps. We see undocumented workers exploited but reviled for supposedly taking away jobs from "real" and "good" citizens.

And we see millions of people—again, disproportionately poor and of color—confronted by (increasingly militarized) police forces and flung into (increasingly privatized) prisons. Given historical and structural racism, poor people of color start the neoliberal race with the least advantage and so are likely to fall behind fastest and furthest. To cope with the armies of the most dramatically dispossessed, neoliberalism has developed a "criminal industrial complex." The War on Drugs, for example, has been waged especially vigorously against poor people of color. Initiated by President Richard Nixon, the War on Drugs was rooted in the soil of racism. H. R. Haldeman, onetime assistant to Nixon, commented that the president "emphasized that you have to face the fact that the whole problem really is the blacks. The key is to devise a system that recognizes this while appearing not to."[45]

Disturbing as all this is, precarity embraces not only the most dramatic or desperate "losers." Many other Americans have not been sucked into the maw of the criminal industrial complex but live with threadbare financial cushions (and are already perilously in debt). The "gig economy," composed of temp workers, Uber drivers, musicians, and others, means that many live not just paycheck to paycheck but gig to gig, without sufficient or any health and other insurance—let alone paid vacations or sick leaves. They may be only one serious accident or illness away from experiencing homelessness.

We still have not gone far enough in recognizing precarity's scope. Run it up the economic ladder another several rungs. Some of us are not fabulously wealthy but do enjoy (relatively) secure jobs and fairly thick financial cushions. Yet even these folks are not free of neoliberal precarity. We are all working harder and longer. And for white-collar workers, benchmarks of job performance are relative rather than absolute. As all workers try harder to beat the current productivity average, workers who fall behind the curve are fired, and only the highest-performing workers remain. "Just because the performance average constantly ratchets up, at some point, unless one can keep pace, one is likely to fall below the average and be let go." By the very virtue of our high performance, we are essentially and constantly working ourselves out of a job: "Everyone is potentially under threat from everyone else. . . . Gains made by coworkers can only portend one's downfall."[46]

45. Duggan, *Twilight of Equality?*, 18.
46. Tanner, *Christianity and the New Spirit*, 178.

If these conditions leave us pitted against coworkers, neoliberal capitalism will certainly allow for little amity between white-collar workers and employers: "Across the board, measures taken by finance-disciplined corporations to maximize profitability prevent workers and employers from profiting together. Thus, even when making outsized profits, corporations cannot risk sharing them with employees by raising wages. Doing so would only cut into company profit margins and thereby threaten the price of company stock."[47]

Nearly all Americans under neoliberalism struggle in a state of precarity. As the theologian Adam Kotsko suggests, "We have to be in a constant state of high alert, always 'hustling' for opportunities and connections, always planning for every contingency (including the inherently unpredictable vagaries of health and longevity). This . . . requires us to fritter away our life with worry and paperwork and supplication, 'pitching' ourselves over and over again, building our 'personal brand'—all for ever-lowering wages or a smattering of piece-work, which barely covers increasingly exorbitant rent, much less student loan payments." (And after all, from a neoliberal perspective, "saddling students with student loans is a highly effective means of forcing them to think about their education in solely economic terms as an investment.")[48]

It is under these conditions of precarity and the frailty of the entrepreneurial self that psychotherapist and pastoral theologian Bruce Rogers-Vaughn speaks of neoliberalism bringing into existence a "third order of suffering." The first two orders of suffering have always been with humanity. The first order is suffering due to the broad human condition: liability to death, grief, separation, illness, natural disaster, and physical pain. The second order arises

---

47. Tanner, 178–79.
48. Kotsko, *Neoliberalism's Demons*, 95 and 119.

from human-on-human evil: war, robbery, rape, murder, and the like. It is the third order that is unique to the neoliberal capitalistic condition. "Diffuse depression," amorphous anxiety, "fluid addictions," and indefinable but intense shame characterize it. "The people I now see," Rogers-Vaughn writes, "tend to manifest a far more diffuse or fragmented sense of self, are frequently more overwhelmed, experience powerful forms of anxiety and depression too vague to be named, display less self-awareness, have often loosened or dropped affiliations with conventional human collectives, and are increasingly haunted by shame rooted in a nebulous sense of personal failure."[49] We have already seen that the entrepreneurial self is atomistically individualistic, fragmented, and insecure. This explains the pressing problems of social disconnection, diffuse depression, and nagging but unclear anxiety Rogers-Vaughn sees in his patients. The hazy yet oppressive sense of shame arises from the neoliberal tendency to allow individuals to blame wholly and only themselves for any and all of their problems.

And in the current environment, we are not shy about shaming others. Precarity has bred abundant sadism in our media entertainment. For neoliberal capitalism, competition is the primary virtue, and solidarity and genuine care for others are signs of weakness, to be ignored or exploited. The flood of reality TV programs in the main center on competition, eventuating in a single winner. The *Apprentice*, the *Bachelor*, *America's Next Top Model*, *Naked and Afraid*, *Hell's Kitchen*, *American Idol*, and a host of others build on this format. But the ne plus ultra of such shows is of course the pioneering *Survivor*, which premiered in 2000.

Survivor always takes place on an island or other isolated area. It imagines a severely austere world of scarce resources. Contestants

49. Rogers-Vaughn, *Caring for Souls*, 126–27 and 2, respectively.

start out on teams but know from the beginning that only a single player will prevail in these harsh circumstances. Thus any posturing about teamwork is just that—posturing that impels the players to jockey for an advantage over one another. Relationships are pawns, manipulated as the players compete with Machiavellian wits and calculating self-presentation. Through a process of elimination via cutthroat entrepreneurialism, finally one player walks away with all the rewards. *Survivor* and its ilk are nothing if not preeminent neoliberal training films.

The sadism comes in not only through complacently watching the suffering of others but by virtue of the fact that such shows often enlist viewers among the judges of the players. In this role, we assume the mantle of neoliberalism's "winners," looking down on competitors from a perch of superior and seemingly untouchable power. We cheer for the most adept manipulators and dismiss the hapless without pity. But the sadism is even harsher with other reality TV, trash-talk and pseudotherapeutic programs such as the *Jerry Springer Show* and *Dr. Phil*. Here ordinary Americans, frequently from the lower classes, divulge to the world the fixes and moral dilemmas they have gotten themselves into: incestuous entanglements, adulterous flings, spectacular addictions, and so forth. Sickly seeking acknowledgment and validation, they offer themselves up "on the altar of abject humiliation" for preachy admonishment and scornful ridicule. This, says Mirowski, is "the unabashed theater of cruelty, the public spaces where we gaze upon the half-speed car wrecks of the lives of others in the throes of failure, Nascar for the politically challenged."[50]

---

50. Mirowski, *Never Let a Serious Crisis*, 133.

THE FIVE CRISES OF NEOLIBERALISM

I have painted neoliberalism's reign in stark colors. It is pervasive and formidable. Neoliberal capitalism is a hegemony, an all-
insinuating dominance of one class, one power over others. But
all hegemonies have cracks, and there, as Leonard Cohen says, is
where the light gets in. Now that it has been in force for more than
a generation, neoliberalism's cracks are showing. In fact, neoliberal
capitalism faces five serious crises.

The epistemological crisis. Unnamed as it prefers to be,
neoliberalism has presented itself as neutral and natural. With the
help of a host of historians, anthropologists, cultural critics, philosophers, and theologians, we now see that it is neither. We are
naming neoliberalism, and with that naming, we are seeing how it
serves particular interests, benefits a small class of citizens, and dev-
astatingly distorts humanity's common life. Neoliberalism can no
longer effectively pretend to be innocent and ultimately benevolent.
Named, it is identified; identified, it can be challenged.

The social crisis. Neoliberalism denies and denigrates social
ties. Its atomistic individualism cannibalizes society and erodes familial bonds, ethnic bonds, and bonds of faith. But still, these run
deep. They are frayed but not eliminated. Out of concern for these
ties, which yet provide humans their richest and most meaningful
experiences, many means of resisting neoliberalism arise.

The moral crisis. As we have seen, neoliberalism at best
ignores justice—including equality—and at worst renders it mean-
ingless. It finds no place for any objective good or goods, moral or
spiritual. Whereas Adam Smith and other earlier liberals "argued
that the market was the best economic system because it enabled
people to be good, that is, rational and therefore productive, Hayek
and Friedman argue that the market is the best economic system

because it makes no judgments about what is good or bad. It simply maximizes freedom understood as consumer choice." Put otherwise, neoliberals believe that a society cannot be both free and just "because any conception of justice would impose someone's values on others."[51] The economic historian Karl Polanyi, writing in 1944 and rubbing shoulders with Mises and Hayek in his native Austria, was prescient. Polanyi said the sovereign, all-encompassing market imagined (and now instituted) by neoliberals "could not exist for any length of time without annihilating the human and natural substance of society; it [would] physically [destroy] and [transform] his surroundings into a wilderness."[52] And not just a wilderness but a nihilistic wilderness where moral and spiritual values would be cannibalized. Yet moral and spiritual goods vitally and profoundly still move and motivate humans of all stripes. Neoliberalism's nihilism begs active resistance.

The demographic crisis. Neoliberalism idolizes an ethic of expressive individualism—an ethic surrendered to the market and viewing morality as a matter of consumer choice. Accordingly, expressivism particularly concerns individual self-expression and self-fulfillment. Given this, it tends to view children as impediments and inhibitions. The expressive individualist wants few and perfect children, if any at all. This aspect of neoliberal capitalism has discouraged sizeable families, and so the individual expressivist culture literally dwindles. It may replenish itself with immigrants. But in time, if these immigrants and their descendants assimilate to expressive individualism, they themselves will no longer reproduce sufficiently to replenish or sustain the population. Or, if they do not assimilate, they will demographically surpass and replace the

51. Jardine, *Making and Unmaking*, 103 and 106.
52. Polanyi, *Great Transformation*, 3.

culture of expressive individualism. Either way, the neoliberal, individual expressivist culture cannot survive.[53]

The ecological crisis. Capitalism has been destructive, but *creatively* destructive (Joseph Schumpeter). Using natural resources to fuel its productive machinery, capitalism has adeptly moved from peat and wood to coal to oil. Now oil is nearly depleted. Can capitalism work another miracle and shift to a new basic energy and fuel source? Perhaps. But even if it does, it has already played a major role in overtaking and cripplingly polluting the earth's atmosphere. The climate crisis, even if further harm were halted tomorrow, will do considerable damage, deleteriously affecting the lives of all humans. Capitalism has been premised on the assumption of infinite growth and ever-rising consumption. In a clearly finite and much-exhausted world, this assumption no longer makes sense. For many, it is clear that we should seek a less heedless, more modest, and sustainable way of life—one that does not simply exploit and plunder nature but recognizes that we are all a part of a web of life that includes the atmosphere, soil, plants, animals, and humans. Neoliberalism, only and always revving for more market rapaciousness and expansion, has nothing to offer in this regard.

In a word, the crisis neoliberalism confronts is one of sustainability. It is not sustainable epistemologically, socially, morally,

---

53. See Jardine, *Making and Unmaking*, 128–29. For now classic philosophical critiques of expressive individualism, see MacIntyre, *After Virtue*; and *Whose Justice?* In addition, note Kotsko, himself young enough to have lived under no regime except neoliberalism, who comments, "It is precisely the generation that has known nothing but neoliberalism that is most likely to reject it. The order that strove to shape the entire world in its image—nay, to reshape human nature itself!—appears to be failing spectacularly in the core task of any political-theological paradigm: ensuring that it is accepted and reproduced by the next generation" (*Neoliberalism's Demons*, 125).

demographically, or ecologically. Yet it remains strong, with committed adherents. Its strange force must be accounted for in another register. It is time to name neoliberal capitalism as a religion.

NEOLIBERALISM AS RELIGION

The cultural critic Walter Benjamin, in a fragment sketched in 1921, sensed the emergence of capitalism as not just an economic system but a faith, a totalizing way of life: "A religion may be discerned in capitalism—that is to say, capitalism serves essentially to allay the same anxieties, torments, and disturbances to which the so-called religions offered answers." He mused further, "Capitalism is the celebration of a cult *sans rêve et sans merci* [without dream or mercy]. There are no 'weekdays.' There is no day that is not a feast day, in the terrible sense that all its sacred pomp is unfolded before us; each day commands the utter fealty of each worshiper." Capitalism was born and grew "as a parasite of Christianity," but as it matured, a great reversal had occurred, so that now "Christianity's history is essentially that of a parasite—that is to say, of capitalism."[54]

Publishing in 2019, the historian Eugene McCarraher takes Benjamin's tantalizing sketch and develops it into a full-blown portrait—indeed, an expansive mural that would cover a building's full wall (McCarraher's book is 679 pages long). McCarraher argues that capitalism is not an agent of disenchantment but a regime of "enchantment, a repression, displacement, and renaming of our intrinsic and inveterate longing for divinity." It is a "parody or perversion of our longing for a sacramental way of being in the world." The "Gospel of Mammonism" is "the meretricious ontology of capital, in which everything receives its values—and even

54. Benjamin, "Capitalism as Religion," 288, 289.

its very existence—through the empty animism of money."[55] The rest of McCarraher's massive (and masterful) book traces capitalist enchantment in America through Puritan foundings that saw business success as an ultimate sign of providential blessing, to a nation with no nobility or established church but with the capitalist marketplace as the new *religio*, to awed and worshipful bowing before the massive turbines of industry, to visions of skyscrapers and department stores as new cathedrals and holy temples, to modern advertising as a kind of evangelism, to Walt Disney's kingdom as the rebirth of totemism and animism, to our present neoliberal dispensation.

I find Benjamin's hints and McCarraher's history largely persuasive, but less sympathetic critics may argue that they have overstated the case. Like the liberal theorist John Rawls, such critics may worry about traditional religions and other "comprehensive doctrines" that purport to take in all of life and life's purposes. They may suggest that liberal capitalism seeks only to ensure the freedom of the market in economic matters and otherwise leave people to themselves and their own preferences. I do not think that counterargument holds, but even if it did, we can stick to our present point of *neoliberal* capitalism. And neoliberalism is nothing if not a comprehensive doctrine.

As we have seen, neoliberalism subordinates all life (human and natural) to the market; its eschatology asserts that neoliberal capitalism is the end point of history, that it provides the best humanity can hope for; and it aims to reshape nothing less than human nature and the whole world. In short, as Kotsko puts it, "Whereas classical liberalism insisted that capitalism had to be allowed free rein within its sphere, under neoliberalism capitalism no longer has a set

55. McCarraher, *Enchantments of Mammon*, 4, 5, 6.

sphere." Neoliberalism asserts itself as "a complete way of life and a holistic worldview, in a way that previous models of capitalism did not." In an especially felicitous insight, Kotsko notes that neoliberalism is a kind of theodicy, "justifying the ways of the economy to man."[56]

Mirowski, to draw another witness into the dock, observes that neoliberal economists "come convinced they possess a Theory of Everything at the End of History, and apply their so-called economic approach to everything great and small under the sun: life and death, sex, neurons, nations, language, knowledge, science itself, personal identity, evolution, aesthetics, global environmental disruption, even human virtues such as dignity." Under neoliberalism, "Economics ceased to be concerned with conventional economic questions, and claimed purview over any all attempts of the agent at self-fashioning: drug addiction, marriage, divorce, suicide, gender bending, religion, theology, abortion, changes in preference." Furthermore, neoliberalism's lionization of risk is "the utter subjection of the self to the market by offering oneself up to powers greater than we can ever fully comprehend, with the parallels to the religious traditions intentional." For

> salvation through the market comes not from solidarity with any delusional social class or occupational category, but instead bold assertion of individuality through capitulation to a life of risk. . . . The neoliberal celebration of risk is woven throughout everyday life in the modern era. For instance, this may explain why casino and commercial gambling has made such a comeback in the neoliberal era. . . . In the neoliberal pantheon, the person who abjectly submits to

---

56. Kotsko, *Neoliberalism's Demons*, 6, 7.

risk (even handicapped by house advantage) is a hero, not a weak-willed fool. Hence, in modern life, and in contrast with prior regimes, gambling takes on an aura of moral probity.[57]

Finally, we can avail ourselves of a papal assist. In his apostolic exhortation *Evangelii Gaudium*, Pope Francis speaks of the "*sacralized* workings of the prevailing economic system" (what we have named as neoliberalism) and denounces the heedless sway of a "*deified* market, which [has] become the only rule."[58] On one (nonofficial) occasion, Francis named neoliberalism explicitly and sharply, saying, "No one can accept the precepts of neoliberalism and consider themselves a Christian."[59] One popular critical reading (the neoconservative) casts Francis as a papal outlier. It is wrong. This pope speaks out of the venerable tradition of Catholic social thought, which has long had its worries about untrammeled capitalism. Francis's immediate two predecessors voiced related concerns, John Paul II in his denunciations of "economism" (subordinating all life to the economy) and Benedict XVI in his teaching on the priority of *caritas*.[60]

It is then no exaggeration to name neoliberalism as a functional religion. Christians need not be hostile to other religions; combat is not the only language for engaging Jews, Muslims, Buddhists, and other adherents of traditional religions. Thus to name neoliberalism as a religion is not in and of itself to condemn it. But it is to say we need to recognize that neoliberal capitalism invites—indeed, demands—theological engagement, because in its

57. Mirowski, *Never Let a Serious Crisis*, 23–24, 114–15, 119, 121–22.

58. Pope Francis, *Evangelii Gaudium*, 2.54 and 2.56 (emphasis added).

59. See Eggemeier and Fritz, *Send Lazarus*, 217n54.

60. Eggemeier and Fritz, 15–61.

comprehensiveness, it is itself a kind of theology. The second part of this book attempts just such engagement. But first, we need to step back and take a fresh account of Christianity and its past, present, and future prospects for being something more than a parasite of capitalism.

3

AFTER APOCALYPSE

We live in a world in catastrophe or always on the edge of catastrophe. Our institutions—political, social, economic, religious—are dangerously eroded, at the cusp of collapse, and it is not clear they can be renewed or what might replace them. The best science sees a world threatened by ecological disaster, with grievous and comprehensive social and political chaos to follow. Pandemics strike to disastrous effect. As Islam asserts itself, some see looming a cataclysmic "clash of civilizations." Even within relatively prosperous and stable states such as America, there is dark talk of imminent civil war.

Since 1914, the West has been in crisis. Two world wars and their awesome ripple effects left an order arguably built in and on conditions of post-traumatic stress disorder (PTSD).[1] Even though fascism and (Soviet) communism did not prevail, perseverating and intrusive memories of them endure, shape governmental and military policies, and bear down on individual lives. Terrorism, whose

---

1. For the argument that the present world order is marked by crisis since 1914, see Reno, *Return of the Strong Gods*. For an illuminating discussion of trauma and its corporate, transgenerational effects, see Charles and Rah, *Unsettling Truths*, 164–95.

historical motivations flow in large part out of policies enacted in the battles with fascism and communism, threatens as an everyday reality and possibility. This possibility contributes to a societal state of anxiety and hypervigilance, another symptom of PTSD. The PTSD survivor is at once haunted by a painful past and dwells in a precarious present with no anticipated relief from the effects of trauma.

A chronic and impending condition of catastrophe incites people to forget the past and imagine no future. The catastrophic atmosphere leaves us only with the fragile present. Some critics of liberalism understand this life in an eternal present as a natural out-growth of liberalism itself. Concerned to free atomistic individuals from the binding ties of tradition, custom, and culture, liberalism robs us all of the past and the future. The political philosopher Patrick Deneen avers that liberalism and its variant progressivism are "grounded in a deep hostility toward the past, particularly tradition and custom. While widely understood to be future-oriented, [they] in fact [rest] on simultaneous assumptions that contemporary solutions must be liberated from past answers but that the future will have as much regard for our present as we have for the past." Consequently, "liberalism makes humanity into mayflies, and unsurprisingly, its culmination has led each generation to accumulate scandalous levels of debt to be left for its children, while rapacious exploitation of resources continues in the progressive belief that future generations will devise a way to deal with the depletions."[2]

If this is true of liberalism, it is especially true of its present variant, neoliberalism, which wants to preempt and settle accounts with the future even while it denigrates the past as primitive and at best vestigial. Riding the market roughshod through all national and

2. Deneen, *Why Liberalism Failed*, 73 and 74.

natural borders, neoliberalism has no respect for place and local culture. And neoliberalism thrives on catastrophe, viewing it as an opportunity to widen and assert the market's reach. (The answer to every crisis, even one apparently induced by the market, is more market dominance.) Neoliberalism's proponents argue that with the pervasive and all-encompassing market, we have arrived at the end of history, having achieved the best humanity can hope for.

In this sense, as well as in its affinity for catastrophe, neoliberalism is apocalyptic. An apocalypse is about endings, and in the popular imagination, those endings are usually violent and hugely destructive. If at all possible, then, they are to be avoided. Yet our present time is one when apocalypse seems all too inevitable. Whatever exact apocalypse will overtake us, we are in the media flooded daily with a succession of possible apocalypses—an ecological crisis, a viral epidemic, a nuclear holocaust, computer network meltdown, a civil war, or an economic collapse. In such a world, one might forgivably think we could do without any other possible sort of apocalypse. Yet in this chapter, I choose to confront apocalypse not with an argument for the elimination of all apocalypses but with a proposal to return to a better, truer, and even promising apocalypse: that of the gospel of Jesus Christ. As we will see, apocalypse need not be all bad. In fact, apocalypse is our only and best hope.

APOCALYPSE ORIGINALLY

In chapter 1, we noted that liberalism owes much to its Jewish and Christian precedents. The same holds true for apocalypse. The very term comes from Jewish and Christian sources, and the expectation that history might have an end and a goal is a Jewish and Christian expectation.

As a literary phenomenon, apocalyptic originated in Judaism in the second century BCE. It arose among a persecuted and oppressed people at a time of frequent martyrdom. It sought to answer questions about the meaning of suffering on a historic scale and where the God of Israel—the maker of heaven and earth and ultimate superintendent of history—was in the midst of that suffering. In short, things were not as they ought to be. Faithful people were suffering. How in turn was God proving faithful?[3]

Apocalypse, in its original Greek, simply means "revelation." The apocalypticists claimed a vision or message from God that revealed how God was ultimately in control of history and the future. At its heart, the Jewish and Christian apocalypse offered a heavenly perspective on earthly reality.[4] The apocalypticists emphasized that God had acted and is acting. All did not depend on human agency. Furthermore, the apocalypticists spoke on a cosmic scale: God was not addressing simply psychological or private individual concerns; God was acting universally, to change the whole world, the course of history, and all of creation with it.

Apocalypticists often expected that God would work through a representative, God's messiah or anointed one. They also often expected that God would work now or at least imminently. If God was intervening in history, to alter its very direction, an apocalypse would create a moment of crisis for those who witnessed and participated in it. They would have an all-important decision to make: Would they now join God and God's work as revealed? Or would they try to ignore or even act against it? Thus a moment of significant, life-changing judgment, implicit or explicit, was ineluctable.[5]

---

3. See Beker, *Paul's Apocalyptic Gospel*, 30.

4. Davies, *Paul among the Apocalypses?*, 45.

5. See O'Regan, *Theology and the Spaces*, 19.

Consider now some entailments of these characteristics of apoc-alyptic. If history and the world have gone wrong, and if God will now act salvifically to change things, God's intervention will appear radical and on an unprecedented scale. It may even be experienced as a kind of salutary invasion, "a rupture of order, a destruction of the familiar, and a halting of life so that nothing remains the same."[6]

We are now in position to quit speaking of apocalyptic generally and turn more definitely to the apocalypse of the gospel of Jesus Christ. Specifically, I mean especially apocalyptic as it was invoked by the apostle Paul, the New Testament's most outstanding apoca-lyptic thinker.

PAUL AND APOCALYPSE

It is first important to place Paul in his Jewish and messianic-Jewish eschatological context. Judaism, and Christianity after it, work on a cosmic scale. With Jesus, the kingdom has been inaugurated, but it has not yet been manifested in its fullness. We look ahead to Jesus's parousia, when God will raise the dead into transformed, new bod-ies (1 Cor 15). More than this, we look ahead to a new heaven and a new earth. The apostle Peter anticipates Jesus's return, which will effect the "*universal restoration* that God announced long ago through his holy prophets" (Acts 3:21). Second Peter 3:13 (NET) similarly declares that "we have [God's] promise" and "are waiting for new heavens and a new earth, in which righteousness truly resides." Rev-elation likewise expects "a new heaven and a new earth" (Rev 21:1) and the New Jerusalem, the city of God that descends to earth, to include a rolling river that nourishes trees of life (Rev 22:2). At the

6. Belcher, "'Discerning the Body,'" 242.

fullness of time, the Letter to the Ephesians says, God "will gather up all things in [Christ], things in heaven and things on earth" (Eph 1:10).

As the New Testament scholar J. Christiaan Beker puts it, "The gospel is not primarily an intrapsychic phenomenon that limits itself to the conversion of individual souls climbing out of a lost world into the safety of the church, like drowning people climb aboard a safe vessel. Rather, the gospel proclaims the new state of affairs that God has initiated in Christ, one that concerns the nations and the creation. Individual souls and their experience are only important within that worldwide context and for the sake of the world."[7]

The apostle Paul accordingly understands the gospel of Jesus Christ working on just this cosmic scale. And he wants his brothers and sisters in the faith to know "that the gospel that was proclaimed by me is not of human origin; for I did not receive it from a human source, nor was I taught it, but I received it through a revelation [*apocalypsis*] of Jesus Christ" (Gal 1:11–12). On the Damascus Road, Paul was seized by an apocalypse that broke time in two—for Jesus "gave himself . . . to set us free from the present evil age" (Gal 1:4).

Time language in Paul exudes the apocalypse of the gospel of Jesus Christ. Stories of Israel's history were written down, Paul observes, "to instruct us, on whom the *ends of the ages have come*" (1 Cor 10:11; emphasis added). In addition, "While we were minors, we were enslaved to the elemental spirits of the world. But when the *fullness of time* had come, God sent his Son, born of a woman, born under the law, in order to redeem those who were under the law, so that we might receive adoption as children" (Gal 4:3–5; emphasis added). Similarly, God's eternal plan awaits the "fullness of time, to gather up all things in [Christ], things in heaven and things on

7. Beker, *Paul the Apostle*, 8.

earth" (Eph 1:10).[8] Now, Paul tells the Corinthians, the "appointed time has grown short," for "the present form of this world is passing away" (1 Cor 7:29, 31). Since the appointed time has drawn near, the Romans are instructed, "Do not be conformed to this world/age, but be transformed by the renewing of your minds" (Rom 12:2). "You know what time it is," Paul says to them, "how it is now the moment for you to wake from sleep. For salvation is nearer to us now than when we became believers; the night is far gone, the day is near" (Rom 13:11–12).

By Paul's lights, Jesus is nothing less than the hinge of history. Before his advent, humanity was enslaved, in darkness, at best to be treated like minors under tutelage and discipline. Now we are liberated and emancipated for maturity and adoption as heirs in the family of God. Even now, in a removed age long separate from Christ's earthly life and highly secularized, our calendars reflect this hinge, with *BC* denoting "before Christ" and *AD* anno Domini, or "in the year of our Lord."[9] Other Jewish apocalypticists expected a messiah on whom the ages would hinge. Paul's apocalyptic thought was distinctive in two major regards.

First, Paul believed the messiah had come in Jesus of Nazareth, something the vast majority of his Jewish contemporaries, to his pain, did not accept. Second, Paul innovatively saw the new age

8. Ephesians is not among the seven letters (Romans, 1 and 2 Corinthians, Galatians, Philippians, 1 Thessalonians, and Philemon) widely accepted as written directly by Paul. However, its eschatology is congruent with the Paul of the seven. Hence I will in this survey include citations from Ephesians. The same can be said for the Letter to the Colossians, also to be cited. See Beker, *Paul the Apostle*, 190; and the discussion of Pauline authorship in Campbell, *Pauline Dogmatics*, 720–24.

9. BCE (before the Common Era) and CE (Common Era) are designations obscuring the Christian origins of the worldwide calendar—but only slightly, for they still pivot on the dates of Jesus's life.

arriving and to unfold in two stages.[10] Other Jewish apocalypticists expected the new age to arrive simultaneously with Israel's liberation from exile and captivity and the resurrection of the dead. (The Pharisees, for example, looked forward to resurrection from death at the coming of the liberating messiah.) Paul believed the new age had commenced with Jesus's life, crucifixion, and resurrection. But still awaiting, only after an interim, was the general resurrection of the dead. *Already*, then, Jesus had defeated the powers of sin, death, and the flesh and ushered in the incipient presence of the kingdom of God on earth. *Not yet*, though, have sin, death, and the flesh been altogether vanquished and the kingdom of God manifested in its fullness. Thus Christians live in a time between the times: between the times of Christ's resurrection and their own, between the times of Christ's first and second comings, between the times of the kingdom's beginnings and its completeness, between the times of Christ's lordship established and revealed and of its acknowledgment by all the peoples of the earth.

For Paul, the in-betweenness of our postapocalyptic existence does not diminish the stunning newness that has decidedly arrived. "So if anyone is in Christ," he writes, "there is a new creation: everything old has passed away; see, everything has become new!" (2 Cor 5:17). And in Galatians 6:15, he declares, "For neither circumcision nor uncircumcision is anything; but a new creation is everything!"

With the advent of Christ, and through his death and resurrection, *everything* has become new. Christ's work has soared to the highest heights and plumbed the deepest depths of all that God made, resulting in an absolutely new, transformed creation. Now nothing—"neither death, nor life, nor angels, nor rulers, nor things

10. Here, see Wright, *Paul and the Faithfulness*, 1043–1265.

present, nor things to come, nor powers, nor height, nor depth, nor anything else in all creation"—can "separate us from the love of God in Christ Jesus our Lord" (Rom 8:38–39). After apocalypse, nothing will go untouched, unrenewed, unrestored.

when

The Galatians text points to a specific aspect of this comprehensive newness. We must remember that biblically, the ultimate gulf separating humankind is that between Jew and Gentile. No more comprehensive division could be imagined than that distinguishing the chosen and circumcised (Jew) from the uncircumcised (Gentile). In our day, we may think of divisions between races, between the sexes, between enemy nations, or in a riven America, between Republicans and Democrats. To the biblical eye, no such division is equal in depth or decisiveness to the division between Jew and Gentile. Yet, says Paul, after Christ, this most profound of distinctions no longer counts. Instead, "new creation is everything!"

The Letter to the Ephesians expands on this theme. Once, the Gentile correspondents are told, you were "aliens from the commonwealth of Israel, and strangers to the covenants of promise, having no hope and without God in the world" (Eph 2:12). But now by the blood of Christ shed on the cross, the Gentiles are included, for Christ has "broken down the dividing wall" between Jew and Gentile (Eph 2:14). Gentiles are no longer lost in the cosmos, vagrants of the universe, without citizenship, but are full members of "the household of God" (Eph 2:19). In place of divided, hostile humanities, there is now one peaceful new humanity, united in and through the body of Christ (Eph 2:15–16).

And if the great divide between Jew and Greek has been undercut and bridged, what of lesser distinctions or separations? Paul reserves none from the apocalyptic sweep. He declares, "There is no longer Jew or Greek, there is no longer slave or free, there is no longer male or female; for all of you are one in Christ Jesus" (Gal

3:28). As New Testament scholar J. Louis Martyn indicates, this means "nothing less than the end of the cosmos" as it was.[11]

We have just seen how there is "no longer Jew or Greek" (Gentile). As for slave and free, the ancient world was starkly hierarchical. Slaves enjoyed few privileges and were liable to pecuniary, physical, and sexual abuse without recourse. The free (and of course especially their masters) lorded over the entirety of their lives. Yet Paul, in light of the apocalyptic gospel, forbids this in the church, where slave and free are on equal footing under Christ. In fact, Paul—a learned free man and a Roman citizen—puts himself on the slaves' level, declaring himself a slave beside them in Jesus Christ (Rom 1:1).

A strict hierarchy also separated male and female. Yet again Paul envisions the apocalypse bridging and obliterating the division. Female as well as male are baptized in Christ, and in this baptism, "the structure of the original creation has been set aside."[12] As the New Testament scholar John Barclay puts it, the gospel has "rendered invalid the social binaries and hierarchies normally taken for granted." By overarching and recontextualizing all distinctions—ethnic, religious, social, economic, sexual—in "content and character, the Christ-event shatters every human paradigm of congruity and connection: it grounds a life that is 'not in accord with human norms' (Gal 1:11), not beholden to schemata of value derived from human history or culture." Elsewhere, Barclay refers to it as a "cosmos-shattering event." For Paul, "new creation" connotes not simply individual conversion but nothing less than "cosmic refashioning."[13]

Paul insists that the new creation is utterly new. For in Christ, God "gives life to the dead and *calls into existence the things that do not*

11. Martyn, *Galatians*, 376.
12. Martyn, 376.
13. Barclay, *Paul and the Gift*, 338, 387, 399, 395, respectively.

exist" (Rom 4:17; emphasis added). Before Christ, there was no one new humanity, there were no Christ-transformed people ready or able to live in Christ's Spirit. As Barclay notes, the persons transformed in and by the gospel are not simply "old selves morally improved, but new creatures forged *ex nihilo* from the resurrection life of Christ."[14] The apocalyptic new creation is no mere adjustment or enhancement of preexisting life. It has been called into being out of nothing with no precedent.

Creation out of nothing is exclusively God's business. But mark also the first phrase in the Pauline text just quoted. Paul says that in Christ, God "gives life to the dead." Resurrection, too, is exclusively God's business. And resurrection is apocalyptic language, making sense only in that context.[15] Wherever in the New Testament resurrection is spoken of, we should recognize over- or undertones of the apocalyptic new creation, the total reconstitution of the cosmos. In Romans especially, Paul emphasizes that Christians are resurrection people. We were dead in sin. In baptism, we die and rise in Christ (Rom 6:1–14). "We know that our old self was crucified with him so that the body of sin might be destroyed, and we might no longer be enslaved to sin" (Rom 6:6). Yet we not only have died in Christ but will "certainly be united with him in a resurrection like his" (Rom 6:5). Nor is resurrection mere resuscitation; it is the raising of the weak, corruptible, physical body as a powerful, incorruptible, spiritual body (1 Cor 15:42–44)—the glorified heir of eternal life, never to die again.

A resurrected human body seems glory and wonder enough. But once again, I must emphasize the comprehensiveness of Paul's apocalyptic vision. Paul connects "the redemption of our bodies"

14. Barclay, 473.
15. Beker, *Paul the Apostle*, 152; and *Paul's Apocalyptic Gospel*, 46.

(Rom 8:23) to the liberation and transformation of the more-than-human creation. The rocks and trees, dogs and bees—all of extrahuman creation "waits with eager longing for the revealing [*apocalypsin*] of the children of God" (Rom 8:19). For now, creation is subject to futility, in bondage to decay, but someday it will "obtain the freedom of the glory of the children of God" (Rom 8:20–21). This is the "universal restoration" Peter preached (Acts 3:21).

If Paul's apocalyptic vision encompasses all of creation, it certainly encompasses the human practice of politics. Paul's Letter to the Romans, written to inhabitants at the very center of imperial power, opens with the bald, nervy recognition that Jesus (implying clearly not Augustus or any other divinized Caesar) is "declared to be Son of God" (Rom 1:4). The philosopher Jacob Taubes comments, "'Son of God' . . . is not a natural quality, but an ascribed quality, as it says in Psalm 2, the coronation psalm, 'You are my son, I have fathered you this day.' This is an act of enthronement. So we are dealing with a conscious emphasis of those attributes that are imperatorial, kingly, imperial. They are stressed before the congregation in Rome, where the imperator [i.e., Caesar] is himself present, and where the center of the cult of the emperor, the emperor religion, is located." Paul addresses the church located at the center of political power, and his words consciously oppose or challenge that power. Taubes continues, "I want to stress that this is a political declaration of war, when a letter using these words . . . is sent to the congregation at Rome to be read aloud. . . . One could, after all, have introduced it pietistically, quietistically, neutrally, or however else. . . . This is why my thesis is that in this sense the Epistle to the Romans is a political theology, a *political* declaration of war on the Caesar."[16]

16. Taubes, *Political Theology of Paul*, 14 and 16. For a robust theological, apocalyptic engagement with Taubes and two atheistic, materialist philosophers (Giorgio

The Letter to the Ephesians is no less bold or sweeping in its politically loaded, apocalyptic claim that "God put this power to work in Christ when he raised him from the dead and seated him at his right hand in the heavenly places, far above all rule and author and power and dominion, and above every name that is named, not only in this age but also in the age to come" (Eph 1:20–21). Consider also Colossians 2:15: through his cross, Christ "disarmed the rulers and authorities and made a public example of them, triumphing over them in it." Apropos both these texts, the theologian Douglas Harink exposits, "The claims to ultimacy and the demands for ultimate allegiance that social and political structures make for themselves are unmasked as the deceptions of false gods. When the true God is revealed in Christ's crucifixion and resurrection, the powers are exposed and defeated, and their ability to deceive is stripped from them."[17]

Philosopher James K. A. Smith nicely captures the gist of these apocalyptic texts:

In short, the political is now inherently eschatological. Christ has disarmed the powers, made a public show of them, and delegitimized their claims to be mediators of ultimacy. "That must be the primary eschatological assertion about the authorities, political and demonic, which govern the world: they have been made subject to God's sovereignty in the Exaltation of Christ. The second, qualifying assertion is that this awaits a final universal presence of Christ to become fully apparent."

Agamben and Alain Badiou) appropriating Paul, see Spaulding, *Just and Loving Gaze.*

17. Harink, *Paul among the Postliberals*, 116.

Everything is *now* in subjection to Christ (Heb. 2:5–8); he has *already* disarmed the principalities and powers (Col. 2:15). But we live in the "not-yet" where this is not universally recognized. It is this *time*—between the cross and kingdom come, between ascension and parousia, between the universal *scope* of his lordship and its universal *recognition*—it is this time or season . . . in which we find ourselves. . . . [Meanwhile,] Earthly rulers remain in place, but their authority is a kind of lame-duck authority.[18]

WHAT'S NEW: EVERYTHING!

Time and all history, new creation ex nihilo, heaven and earth, renewed nature, worldwide politics—the comprehensiveness of the apocalyptic gospel can hardly be overstated. It takes some doing for it to sink in. For aid in that sinking in, I turn to a novel, Emma Donoghue's wondrously imaginative but entirely realistic *Room*.

The story concerns five-year-old Jack and his mother. She was kidnapped by an evil man called Old Nick when she was nineteen. Old Nick imprisons Ma in an eleven-by-eleven-foot outbuilding in his backyard. There is a skylight and a television. Otherwise, she has been shut off from all connection to the outside world.

Old Nick repeatedly visits and rapes Ma. After some three years in captivity, she conceives and births Jack. The story opens just as Jack is turning five. Jack's reality is the eleven-by-eleven-foot room. With little else to do, Ma has taught Jack how to read and work numbers. He is a precociously articulate little boy and the novel's sole narrator.

---

18. Smith, *Awaiting the King*, 79 and 159 (internal quotation from Oliver O'Donovan).

Mountains are something Jack has only seen on TV, and they are "too big to be real."[19] So too are forests "and also jungles and deserts and streets and skyscrapers and cars. Animals are TV except ants and Spider and Mouse, but he's gone back now. Germs are real, and blood. Boys are TV but they kind of look like me, the me in Mirror that isn't real either, just a picture."[20] Men "aren't real except Old Nick, and I'm not actually sure if he's real for real. Maybe half? He brings groceries and Sundaytreat and disappears the trash, but he's not human like us. He only happens in the night, like bats."[21]

For Jack, TV shows different imaginary "planets." So there's a game show planet "where people win prizes" and another planet "where women hold up necklaces and say how exquisite they are."[22] But when Jack turns five, Ma decides he is old enough to know that what the TV pictures is (often) real. He guesses she "was sort of lying" to him before. Now she's "unlying."[23] She tells Jack, "Listen. What we see on TV is . . . it's pictures of real things." Jack is flabbergasted. "That's the most astonishing thing I ever heard," he thinks.[24]

Jack wonders how TV can be pictures of real things. He struggles to take it in: "I think about them all floating around in Outside Space outside the walls, the couch and the necklaces and the bread and the killers and the airplanes and all the shes and hes, the boxers and the man with one leg and the puffy-hair woman, they're

19. Donoghue, *Room*, 18.
20. Donoghue, 54.
21. Donoghue, 18.
22. Donoghue, 61.
23. Donoghue, 85.
24. Donoghue, 59.

floating past Skylight."[25] His sense of reality is shaken to the core: "Room is real for real, but maybe Outside is too only it's got a cloak of invisibility on like Prince JackerJack in the story. Baby Jesus is TV I think except the painting with his Ma and his cousin and his Grandma, but God is real looking in Skylight with his yellow face, only not today, there's only gray."[26]

Jack decides, "Outside has everything. Whenever I think of a thing now like skis or fireworks or islands or elevators or yo-yos, I have to remember they're real, they're actually happening in Outside all together. It makes my head tired. And people too, firefighters teachers burglars babies saints soccer players and all sorts, they're all really in Outside. I'm not there, though, me and Ma, we're the only ones not there. Are we still real?"[27]

Ma has thought about escape for years but has never managed it. With Jack maturing, she's all the more desperate to break free. It's one thing to have a baby in a confined space, but now the baby's growing up. "You don't even know what it's doing to you," she tells her boy. "You need to see things, touch things—" But Jack is ambivalent about escaping Room, all the world he's ever known. He objects, "'Room's not small. Look.' I climb up on my chair and jump with my arms out and spin, I don't bang into anything."[28]

Eventually, Ma hatches a plan, and with help, they escape. Much of the rest of the novel then concerns Jack's adjustment to the outside. We see him encounter his first vending machine, his first automatic toilet, his first hand dryer, his first aquarium, his first time on stairs, his first shoes, his first time outside in the daytime, his

25. Donoghue, 61–62.
26. Donoghue, 63–64.
27. Donoghue, 70–71.
28. Donoghue, 113.

first computer, his first raindrops, his first car wash, his first time on the beach, his first escalator.[29] All of this is disorienting and overwhelming. Jack's eyes have to adjust to seeing long distances. He has difficulty with spatial perception and filtering and sorting all the whole-body stimuli coming at him.

There are many more sounds, which often make him jump. The first time wind smacks his face, he thinks it may rip him open. Being touched by people other than Ma is "like electric shocks."[30] Once, after a short absence, Ma greets Jack with the common expression, "What's new?"

"Everything," says Jack.[31]

Despite all the disorientation, Jack gradually adjusts and sorts out his new reality. By the end of the book, after just two or three weeks outside, Jack and Ma go back to the room of their captivity. Formerly, Jack was habituated to it and even fond of it. Now it seems impossibly cramped and drab. Jack readily says goodbye to it.

After apocalypse, we are in a situation similar to Jack's. New creation means that *everything* is new, fresh, revolutionary. Like Jack, we may at first find this overwhelming. But soon we adjust: we learn to see everything in the all-revealing light of Christ's death and resurrection, into which we are called to participate. No aspect of our world is untouched—not nature, not our fellow humanity, not politics and all of history.

Like Jack, who has to learn long vision and depth perception, our "eyes" too have to adjust. We have to learn what J. Louis Martyn calls "bifocal vision." Through one focus, we see the "present evil age." We are not unrealistic. We are not blind to suffering

29. Donoghue, 159–60, 162, 163–64, 176, 186, 197, 219, 240, 286, 290–91, 294.
30. Donoghue, 181, 197, 239.
31. Donoghue, 271.

and failure and evil. We know that the church itself can grievously consent to sin and unnecessarily fear death. But through the other focus, which grows ever more intense, we see by the new age. We see that God's power apocalypsed in Christ is "'much more' than the power of Sin, [which] causes God's apocalyptic seer to see the powers of the new creation 'much more' than he sees those of the [passing] Old Age (Rom 5:12–21)."[32] Put otherwise, we see bifocally through the already and the not yet. Already Christ has conquered and liberated, but his victory is not yet universally recognized and acknowledged. The church lives in tension and, until the parousia, is in for a fight with the powers of sin and death.

Finally, like Jack, we learn only retrospectively how cramped, drab, and even hopeless our old world was. Once Jack is outside the room, he is open to a wider world, a new reality that is grander than anything he had previously imagined. Once we are grasped by the apocalyptic gospel, we too look back and see our old reality in a new, more expansive light. Our epistemology or way of knowing is in this sense retrospective, or backward looking. Now freed and looking back, we see that "humanity is trapped, enslaved under hostile forces, and clearly powerless to do anything about it." It is "only in the light of this [apocalyptic] event [that] the truth about the pre-Christian situation [is] actually revealed, along with the truth of the nature of its solution."[33] In other words, Paul the apocalyptic theologian reasons not from plight to solution but from solution to plight.[34] As the theologian Douglas Campbell puts it, "Converts are, in effect, shifted into the new, Christian state in an

---

32. Martyn, *Galatians*, 104.

33. Campbell, *Deliverance of God*, 65, 66.

34. Campbell, 439. This retrospective epistemology, reasoning from Christ's victory (solution) to an understanding of our predicament of enslavement to sin and

event of grace—the apocalyptic moment of revelation—and so look back on the problems from which they have been rescued, reaching new definitions of them. A more objective understanding is now possible with the mind freed from the deceptions and constraints of Sin."[35]

FREEDOM AFTER APOCALYPSE

With an apocalyptic, retrospective epistemology in hand, we can now return to a premier theme of chapters 1 and 2: freedom.

We have noted that neoliberalism (and liberalism in general) is big on negative freedom, freedom *from*. Liberalisms seek to free us from the past and communal, traditional, customary constraints. Thus insofar as we are liberals, we yearn to live without a story. Yet our ties—of faith, birth, place, home—are exactly what make us who we are. We need some way to claim and own these identity- and person-constituting ties, if not being totally determined by them.

Furthermore, liberalism's negative freedom leaves us without positive freedom, freedom *for*. As Stanley Hauerwas observes, "We have made 'freedom of the individual' an end in itself and have ignored the fact that most of us do not have the slightest idea of what we should do with our freedom."[36]

So what is freedom, apocalyptically interpreted?

---

death (plight), is an effective and exciting theme throughout Karl Barth's *Church Dogmatics*.

35. Campbell, *Deliverance of God*, 903.

36. Hauerwas, "Church and Liberal Democracy," 80. Similarly, Paul Babie and Michael Trainor note, "Neoliberalism gives us, then, choice on steroids: choice, yes, but with little, indeed, no, regard for and no guidance as to how it is exercised and how it might go wrong" (*Neoliberalism and the Biblical Voice*, 29).

It is negative freedom, freedom *from*. We have been liberated from the powers of sin and death, and that marvelously. As New Testament scholar Susan Grove Eastman writes, sin and death enslave: "The result for subjective experience is a vicious circle of culpability and compulsion, from which humanity cannot free itself. The human predicament therefore requires more than forgiveness pronounced from on high; it requires a rescue operation on the ground." And that is exactly what the incarnation and Christ's saving life, death, and resurrection enact: "Christ's death with and for us is an 'inside job,' which frees us in an utterly counterintuitive way. He takes the form of a slave; he becomes one of the captives; he joins them in the prison cell; he assumes the position of powerless trust in the God who alone can save. He dies as one of us. He waits for resurrection, which is always God's deed (1 Cor 15:4; Phil 2:9)."[37]

Apocalyptic freedom is also freedom from what Martyn calls the "Impulsive Desire of the Flesh."[38] Enmeshed in sin, we turn in on ourselves and are estranged from others. The "works of the flesh" listed by Paul include "fornication, impurity, licentiousness, idolatry, sorcery, enmities, strife, jealousy, anger, quarrels, dissensions, factions, envy, drunkenness, carousing" (Gal 5:19–21). Note that most of the "works" listed—enmities, strife, jealousy, anger, quarrels, dissensions, factions, envy—obviously hinder corporate life and rip the communal fabric. (The others indirectly do the same.) "By contrast," writes Paul, "the fruit of the Spirit is love, joy, peace, patience, kindness, generosity, faithfulness, gentleness, and self-control" (Gal 5:22–23)—qualities that build and mend the communal body. The apocalyptic gospel frees us from the works that estrange and leave us isolated and threatened.

---

37. Eastman, "Apocalypse and Incarnation," 170 and 171.
38. Martyn, *Galatians*, at, e.g., 447, 485, 492–93, 497, 500.

No less does it free us from our estrangement from God. The source of all life and goodness and beauty and truth is our highest good, and alone will fulfill our deepest human nature. As we have seen, Gentiles were formerly lost in the cosmos, without citizenship in the God of Israel's house. Christ's death reconciles us—Jew and Gentile, the entirety of humanity—to this God. Our broken communion with God is restored in Christ.

Additionally, the apocalyptic gospel rescues us from death, what Paul calls the "last enemy" (1 Cor 15:26). Death would separate us from God (the source and sustainer of life) and one another. Death is the ultimate weapon in the arsenal of Satan and oppressive worldly rulers. Yet Paul declares that Christ has overcome it, that Christians can brave martyrdom in hope of the resurrection, and that eternal life is ultimately our bequest.

So the negative, liberating freedom of Christ's apocalypse is no mean thing. It rescues or delivers us from estrangement with God, with one another, from sin and death and the "Impulsive Desire of the Flesh." But the same apocalypse also points to positive freedom, freedom *for*.

Most of all, we are freed for relationality and communion. God in Christ "drew us back into full personhood, which means into full, authentic, healthy relationality. . . . When that communion has been disrupted he restores it—patiently, gently, and inexorably. When that communion is reestablished he nurtures and deepens it, which means enhancing its relationships. . . . The church is meant to be at bottom an entering into and living within the loving relationality of God."[39]

As Martyn insists, "Freedom, then, is neither an abstraction nor a thing that an individual can possess as though it were a right.

39. Campbell, *Paul*, 62.

Freedom is the condition given by God in the realm of deliverance from slavery, the space God has created by calling the church into being."[40] Christians are to look out for one another, to place the other's interests higher than their own. Positive freedom is freedom for service (Paul calls it slavery) to the neighbor (Gal 5:13).

This may sound onerous. But underlying it all is a resounding reciprocity.[41] I can try to have my back, but how much more effective is it if several others have my back? I am reminded of J. R. R. Tolkien's hobbits and their birthday custom. Rather than the individual hobbit receiving gifts on their birthday, the hobbit gives gifts to all of their neighbors. So many more gifts to be received then—not just on your own birthday but on all the birthdays of your neighbors. I think Paul would find hobbit customs amenable to the spirit of his own call to look first to the neighbor's needs.

And though the bonds with one's fellow church members are especially sure and strong, the apocalyptic gospel reaches beyond the church. Christians, after all, are called to love all their neighbors and even their enemies, whether or not they are fellow Christians. And we are in solidarity no less with nonhuman creation. "We are freed not only *from* sin but also *for* love (Gal. 5:13)," writes Beker. "Freedom's negative aspect is inherent in the defeat of the powers, that is, in our freedom from the power structures of the old age through the intervention of God's act in Christ. And freedom's 'affirmation' stresses our present status in Christ that frees us to serve our neighbor in love and makes us sigh for the freedom of the creation from death in the coming glory of God."[42]

40. Martyn, *Galatians*, 447.

41. On gift/grace and reciprocity, see Barclay's unsurpassed *Paul and the Gift*. See also the excellent treatment in deSilva, *Honor, Patronage*, 121–56.

42. Beker, *Paul the Apostle*, 270–71, citing Rom 8; 1 Cor 9:19–23; and Gal 5:13–15.

Finally, as regards positive freedom, a word about capacitation or enablement. In the thrall of sin and death, we are not free to love God, to love creation, to love others, or even to love ourselves rightly. We are dead in the condition of sin, and only God's Word and God's Spirit can raise us to life and fulsome agency. Resurrection, I have said, is exclusively God's business. So it is only in the Spirit that we are freed for love in all its forms and directions. Through Word and Spirit, we are enabled and given the capacity to love.

Consider an alcoholic turned loose in a liquor store and given free rein to drink whatever and as much as he would like. He has full, but only negative, freedom, in that he is not forbidden any bottle in the store. But he is a slave to his impulses or compulsion. As Alcoholics Anonymous would have it, he needs a "higher power" for true freedom, the freedom not to drink but to live free of bondage and addiction.

Likewise, we are all addicted to sin. It is the Holy Spirit that can give us the capacity not to sin. Our final and fullest freedom, as Augustine would have it, is the freedom not even to be able to sin, but only to love. This is freedom *for*—freedom for love of God, of creation, of others, and truly of ourselves. Such freedom is what the apocalyptic gospel promises.

GOD'S INITIATIVE AND WORLDLY SOLIDARITY

The apocalyptic interpreter Beverly Gaventa concisely summarizes the apocalyptic gospel: "Paul's apocalyptic theology has to do with the conviction that in the death and resurrection of Jesus Christ, God has invaded the world as it is, thereby revealing the world's utter distortion and foolishness, reclaiming the world, and inaugurating a battle that will doubtless culminate in the triumph of

God over all God's enemies (including the captors Sin and Death). This means that the Gospel is first, last, and always about God's powerful and gracious initiative."[43]

We can hardly overemphasize God's initiative. "Not only must God alone do it; God alone has done it," says theologian Philip Ziegler.[44] "As Matthew Boulton observes, commenting on John Calvin's vision of Christian formation, 'the church's practices are fundamentally divine works of descent and accommodation, not human works of ascent and transcendence.'"[45] Theologian Phillip Cary declares, "In place of human spirituality bringing us to God in a kind of ascent of heart and mind, the Gospel tells the story of a divine carnality, a descent of God to us." The gospel of Jesus Christ "announces the defeat of death itself, the glorification of our human bodies, and the renewal of the whole material world rather than escape from it." Speaking of New Testament believers, Cary writes, "Going up to heaven is not what they're looking for, but rather the resurrection of their bodies when heaven comes down to earth."[46] As Karl Barth thrillingly depicts the gospel story, God in Christ has journeyed to us, into the far country, to reconcile us to himself, to confront the deadly and deadening powers, to bring all creation to its true goal.[47]

The church in itself is not the end of this story. Rather, God has established the church as a means of the cosmos-encompassing kingdom he has initiated and will bring to its full manifestation and completeness. The church, meanwhile, is a kind of vanguard,

---

43. Gaventa, *Our Mother Saint Paul*, 81.
44. Ziegler, *Militant Grace*, 90.
45. Cited in Smith, *Imagining the Kingdom*, 15.
46. Cary, *Meaning of Protestant Theology*, 6, 42, 55.
47. Barth, *Church Dogmatics* IV/1 and 2.

a beachhead in besieged creation, an avant-garde proclaiming the magnificent work of God in Christ. Sometimes the church must protest the world's errant ways, but fundamentally, the church is in solidarity with the world and all creation. As Beker insists, Paul's apocalyptic comprehensiveness allows "no dualism between the human soul and the external world. He places the human being in the context of the world and its power struggles. . . . In other words, the various parts of the created world are mutually related to each other and form a united whole. This means that, until all of God's creation comes to its destiny of glory, neither God himself is vindicated nor the human being completely or fully 'saved.'" (I take it that this is something of what Paul means when he comments, "For salvation is nearer to us now than when we became believers" [Rom 13:11].) So "long as creation groans, Christians groan as well." All this "means concretely that our neighbors in the world are persons who not only need us but whom we need as well."[48]

The apocalyptic stance, grounding us in solidarity, provides a different vantage point from which we view our enemies. "The gospel is the great equalizer; we are all in some degree or other enslaved by the malign forces that are set against God. Therefore we regard human beings as enemies only in a provisional, penultimate sense," wisely comments pastor Fleming Rutledge.[49] In Paul's words, "For our struggle is not against enemies of blood and flesh, but against the rulers, against the authorities, against the cosmic powers of this present darkness" (Eph 6:12).

God's initiative, then, and solidarity with all creation. These dual bases equip us to judiciously engage the powers and relate properly to our fellow humanity. We remember that every neighbor (even

---

48. Beker, *Paul's Apocalyptic Gospel*, 36, 37, 110.
49. Rutledge, *Advent*, 20.

every enemy) is someone for whom Christ died. We look first and finally to God's intervention and emphasize that it is God's initiative. Such will rescue us from misguided, insular pride and prevent us from heroic but easily frustrated efforts to save the world all on our own. As Beker writes, unless we view our efforts against the horizon of God's initiative, we too readily succumb to

> a romantic exaggeration of the ethical capability of Christians. . . . In other words, unless Christians know that their ethical activity is essentially an anticipation of that greater reality of God's coming kingdom, they cannot but wonder about the futility of their efforts in view of the overwhelming structures of evil and suffering in our world. And unless Christians know that it is their task to establish nothing but beachheads of the kingdom of God in this world, then not only the sheer magnitude of the ethical task will suffocate them, but also their frequent inability to measure ethical progress will stifle them.[50]

In the course of this book so far, we have traced liberalism and introduced its now reigning variation, neoliberalism. In this chapter, we have outlined the apocalyptic gospel. It remains to unpack the freedoms *from* and freedoms *for* of Christ's apocalypse in confrontation with neoliberalism. The challenge is considerable. But the hope, in light of Christ's life, death, and resurrection, is greater still.

50. Beker, *Paul's Apocalyptic Gospel*, 86–87.

4

FREED FROM THE OVERWEENING MARKET, FREED FOR COVENANT

For neoliberalism, the economy just is the market. And all of life is to be made over in the market's competitive nature. But at its historical roots and through much of history, the economy was broader and deeper than the market. The origins of the word *economy* derive from the Greek *oikonomia*, with *oikos* meaning "household" and *nomia* planted in *nemein*, which translates to "management and dispensation."[1] A household in the Greco-Roman world was typically more expansive than our nuclear family. It consisted of husband and wife, children, some of what we would call "extended family," and slaves. Household management might involve dealings with a market outside its doors, but the *oikos* was most often itself a manufacturing unit that supplied much of its own food, clothing, and other needs.

Over time, *oikonomia* "became a loanword applying to nearly every sphere of life." Wherever people thoughtfully or rationally

1. See Leshem, "What Did the Ancient Greeks?"

planned and managed their energies and their resources—from bodily functions to ethical choices—they were said to be economizing. The universe itself was conceived to be economized by nature.[2]

How broad could the economy be, then? It might be applied to nothing less than the mystery of God and God's intentions for creation. This is largely lost to most of our English translations of the Bible. Consider Ephesians 1:9–10: "[God] has made known to us the mystery of his will, according to his good pleasure that he set forth in Christ, as a plan [in Greek, *oikonomia*] for the fullness of time, to gather up all things in him, things in heaven and things on earth."

Contrast this with the political and economic historian Dotan Leshem's translation, which renders *oikonomia* more precisely than the prosaic *plan*: "He made known to us the mystery of His will, according to His kind intention which He purposed in [Christ]; with a view to an economy of the fullness of ages to recapitulate all in Christ, things in the heavens and things on the earth."[3]

Two aspects jump out from the text.

First, God's economy is comprehensive: it includes all things in the heavens and on the earth. All creatures, all that God has made, have been recapitulated—taken up into and transformed—by Christ's life, death, and resurrection. Everything, to the end of its flourishing, secures its place in God's economy through Christ. We find other echoes of this encompassing, benevolent economy elsewhere in Paul. In Romans 8:18–25, all creation is groaning for release from its bondage to decay through "the freedom of the

2. Leshem.

3. Leshem, *Origins of Neoliberalism*, 25. See also Eph 3:9: "The plan [*oikonomia*] of the mystery hidden for ages."

glory of the children of God" (v. 21). And in Colossians 1:15–20, we read,

> [Christ] is the image of the invisible God, the firstborn of all creation; for in him all things in heaven and on earth were created, things visible and invisible, whether thrones or dominions or rulers or powers—all things have been created through him and for him. He himself is before all things, and in him all things hold together. He is the head of the body, the church; he is the beginning, the firstborn from the dead, so that he might come to have first place in everything. For in him all the fullness of God was pleased to dwell, and through him God was pleased to reconcile to himself all things, whether on earth or in heaven, by making peace through the blood of his cross.

Second, this economy is apocalyptic. It has occurred and been revealed in "the fullness of time." As we saw in chapter 3, "the fullness of time" is code for apocalyptic. The economy or plan of history shows and is enacted in the great ministry of Jesus Christ, by God's timing. History spikes and, as if under a flash X-ray, displays its defining skeletal outline via the overcoming light of Christ. History's consummation has arrived and will be completed at the parousia.

In the time between the times, this apocalyptic and benevolent economy is especially seen in the church. As Paul writes a little further on in the first chapter of his Letter to the Ephesians, "[God] has put all things under [Christ's] feet and has made him the head over all things for the church, which is his body, the fullness of him who fills all in all" (Eph 1:22–23). Building on texts such as this, the church fathers saw politics as the realm where

Caesar coerces through positive and negative incentives. By way of contrast, the apocalyptic economy embodied by the church "becomes a sphere of freedom. This freedom is not the negative freedom that will characterize our modern economy, namely, freedom from political coercion. Instead, it is the positive freedom to pursue the ideal mode of life in the bounds of the economic sphere."[4]

Thus the church and its *oikonomia* are central to any Christian account of economy and its ultimate, proper functioning.

THE CHURCH AS FIRST FAMILY

It is hard to overstate the importance of biological or consanguineous family in the Old Testament and the Jewish world of Jesus's day. In the Old Testament, there was no Hebrew word for *bachelor*, the eunuch was impure, and the barren woman could hardly imagine a reason to go on living (see 1 Sam 1:3–8). Even ascetics such as priests or Nazirites were not single (Lev 21:1–14; Num 6:1–21). Not getting married and bearing children was catastrophic (see Isa 4:1).

In Jesus's place and time, procreation was an obligation and a duty; sometimes a minimum number of children was specified. Rabbi Abba declared that one question sure to be asked at the judgment would be, "Did you engage in procreation?" To be unmarried at the age of twenty was to transgress a commandment of God. Not bearing children was equated with shedding blood and diminishing the image of God.[5]

4. Leshem, *Origins of Neoliberalism*, 129.
5. See Borg, *Jesus*, 122n75; and Malina, *New Testament World*, 133. On procreation and rabbinical views, see Yarbrough, *Not like the Gentiles*, 21–23.

Jesus, single and celibate, broke into this world apocalyptically.[6] He proclaimed, "The time is fulfilled, and the kingdom of God has come near; repent, and believe in the good news" (Mark 1:15). This apocalyptic note is later affirmed by Paul, who says that in Jesus, "the fullness of time had come" (Gal 4:4). Jesus's life, death, and resurrection marked the end of the old age and the beginning of the new (1 Cor 10:11). And the new creation made all things new, including marriage and consanguineous family.

Jesus's teachings in this respect were profoundly shocking. He said that his apocalyptic coming meant that siblings can turn against one another, children against parents, and parents against children (Matt 10:21). He goes so far as to say that, inasmuch as consanguineous family is concerned, "I have come not to bring peace, but a sword" (Matt 10:34). Those who love their father or mother more than Jesus, Jesus says, are not worthy of him (Matt 10:37). He calls an earnest inquirer to leave off burying his father and immediately follow him (Matt 8:21–22; Luke 9:59–62).[7]

6. Dale Allison, remarking on the long and often circuitous road scholarly questers after the historical Jesus have followed, concludes that there is no escaping the apocalyptic context of Jesus's life and message: "Our choice is not between an apocalyptic Jesus and some other Jesus; it is between an apocalyptic Jesus and no Jesus at all" (*Constructing Jesus*, 46–47). Consider also the blunt assertion of Jacob Taubes: "Jesus is not the initiator of something new, but is to be regarded as a phenomenon within the apocalyptic movement in Israel" (*Occidental Eschatology*, 48).

7. Theologian Willie James Jennings starkly retains the startling effect of Jesus's teaching and actions on consanguineous family: "Jesus, in an act of utter terrorism, tore open ancient kinship networks, and now the Spirit will complete that work by forming the new family" (*Acts*, 54). Jennings goes on to warn against marriages that focus primarily on the couple and its hermetic world, not open to hospitality, turning "toward the narcissism of the two made one" (55).

Jesus was saying that the kingdom of God was owed our first and highest allegiance. Nothing—even something as precious and beloved as family—can come before or be more central than the kingdom. At the same time, he did not seek to destroy or eliminate consanguineous family. He affirmed the existence of the family by grounding it in creation and speaking strenuously against divorce (Matt 19:3–12). He welcomed children and recognized the importance of their nurture, desiring to bless them (Mark 10:13–16; Luke 18:15–17). He called his disciples to welcome children just as they welcomed him (Mark 9:37). He also condemned the abusive use of the corban oath, a means through which irresponsible children of elderly parents might defraud them of wealth and care (Mark 7:9–13).[8]

What Jesus did was decenter and relativize consanguineous family. For his followers, the church is to become their first family. So in the Gospel of Mark, in the middle of a teaching session, he can turn away his biological mother and siblings, insisting that "whoever does the will of God is my brother and sister and mother" (Mark 3:35). He promises those deprived of consanguineous family that they will receive houses, siblings, mothers, and children by a hundredfold through the community of his followers (Mark 10:29–31). At the cross, he declares "the disciple whom he loved" to be the son of his mother, Mary, and Mary to be the disciple's mother. "And from that hour," John tells us, "the disciple took her into his own home" (John 19:25–27).

Jesus saw the church, not the consanguineous family, as the vehicle or medium of salvation. He expected the first family, the family of the kingdom, to grow evangelistically rather than biologically (Matt 28:19–20). Entrance to the kingdom and the church witnessing to

---

8. For more detail on corban, see my *Families at the Crossroads*, 78.

it in fact required a second birth, this time of water and the Spirit (John 3:5–6).

Put differently, after the apocalypse, even the most intimate and "natural" relationships do not stand on their own. They are all now mediated through Christ and Christ's body, the church. The great German theologian Dietrich Bonhoeffer writes, "Ever since Jesus called, there are no longer natural, historical, or experiential unmediated relationships for his disciples. Christ the mediator stands between son and father, between husband and wife, between individual and nation, whether they can recognize him or not. There is no way from us to others than the path through Christ, his word, and our following him."[9]

These are the gospel foundations Paul builds on to paint his picture of the church as the first family. Baptism, for Paul, brings death and new life in Christ (Rom 6:1–14). Christians are the (adopted) children of God and siblings to one another (as at 1 Thess 1:4).[10] Paul uses the phrase "my brothers" more than sixty-five times in his letters. He can also call members of a church "my children" (1 Cor 4:14; Gal 4:19). Both the number and the intensity of these familial phrases make Paul's writing remarkable in its time and place. And note the centrality of the Eucharist in Paul, where the church family, like any healthy family, frequently shares meals together (1 Cor 11:17–34).

Thus for the earliest Christians, the church was, like the consanguineous family, a space of birth. Just as the consanguineous family rears and socializes its children, the church (re)socializes persons as first and foremost Christ followers. And just as the consanguineous

9. Bonhoeffer, *Discipleship*, 95.
10. On the central significance of Christians as siblings to one another, see Horrell, *Solidarity and Difference*, 121–26.

family unconditionally cares for its charges, the church calls its multitude of siblings to look out for and attend to the needs of one another.[11] In all these ways, the church, like the consanguineous family, is an *oikos* with an *oikonomia*, a household with an economy.

For Christians, in the economy after the apocalypse, marriage is honorable but no longer obligatory. Singleness has a new and highly honorable status. Because with the apocalypse, the world's possessions, joys, and business have been revealed for what they are. They are good, but they are not ultimately good because they are "passing away" (1 Cor 7:31). The single Christian, compared to the married Christian, will live and serve in less complicated "devotion to the Lord" (1 Cor 7:35). As Stanley Hauerwas comments of singleness, "There can be no more radical act than this, as it is the clearest institutional expression that one's future is not guaranteed by the family, but by the church. The church, that harbinger of the Kingdom of God, is now the source of our primary loyalty."[12] If singles live on, it will be because there is a resurrection. And if they are remembered, they will be remembered by the family called church. Christian singles are thus radical witnesses to the resurrection. They forfeit heirs—the only other possibility of their survival beyond the grave—in the hope that one day, all creation will be renewed.[13]

---

11. David deSilva reminds us that in the Jewish and Greco-Roman ethos of the New Testament, the honor and needs of the family as a whole were to be upheld even at cost to any individual members. This meant that sibling rivalry and ignoring the needs (material as well as spiritual) of a family member were marked as serious vices. This ethos was transferred into the church as new family, with all believers understood as children of one Father (God) and (ideally) as loving, mutually caring siblings to one another. deSilva, *Honor, Patronage*, 157–239.

12. Hauerwas, "Church in a Divided World," 190.

13. On how discipleship troubles (consanguineous) kinship and averts the "tragedy of childlessness," see Banner, *Ethics of Everyday Life*, 35–59.

Meanwhile, married Christians bear children to witness to the church's conviction that God has not given up and will not give up on God's creation. Christians have children because they believe the world has a future. And they have children to witness to and practice hospitality, for no strangers can challenge us so much as the intimate strangers we call children.[14]

COVENANT AND CONTRACT

Closely related to kinship is the key biblical theme of covenant. Covenant gains "much of its character and force . . . from family relations."[15] In marriage, two people covenant to each other (and to God and their community). In addition, in the biblical world, covenant through oath or promise can extend kinship—as to aliens in the land. In this regard, covenant is a kind of adoption. Paul makes use of such customs and concepts in his discussion of the Gentiles' adoption into the family of God (Gal 4:1–7).

Ultimately, the Israelites covenant not just with one another but with God. This is the very God who chose them and set his heart upon them before and apart from any moral merit or size and strength of their population. This is the very God who freed them from slavery in Egypt and gifted them with the promised land. And significantly, this is the very God who created heaven and earth and is Lord of the nations and the course of history.

Consequently, the covenant tie between God and Israel is not a relationship of equals. It is humanly modeled on ancient Near

---

14. For more on children as strangers, see my *Families at the Crossroads*, 133–48. For an immersive tour of the strong theme of marriage in Scripture and the Christian tradition, see Levering, *Engaging the Doctrine*.

15. Levenson, *Love of God*, 22.

Eastern customs of a kind of treaty between a suzerain (a king, the most powerful actor in the relationship) and his vassal. The suzerain expects the whole- and single-hearted allegiance and loyalty of his vassal; the vassal can be absolutely relied on as an ally, not willing to defect to the service of any of the king's enemies. In return, the suzerain owes his vassal protection, succor, and if necessary, rescue from enemies.[16]

But the covenant, if not between equals, is one of genuine and profound love. For God's part, God initiates and commits to his people with ardor and steadfastness. For their part, the people respond in gratitude and with obedience. This is an enactment of a love that is "more outward, action-oriented, and practical than the [sentimental] one that has come to dominate modern Western culture."[17] For both parties, it most resembles the love between parents and children, where parents demonstrate real love not just by professing warm feelings but by feeding, clothing, and otherwise providing for their children via substantial and ongoing deeds of care. If that is what the love of healthy or "good enough" parents looks like, that of "good enough" children includes listening to, following, and respecting trustworthy parents.

Accordingly, in the biblical world, covenant was not made just or primarily on the basis of blood. To be a son or daughter was first of all, in Hebrew thought, to be obedient, not to indicate biological descent. Israel's election as the "children of God" entailed obedience (Deut 13:17–14:2). If Israel disobeyed, God might spurn "his sons and daughters" (Deut 32:19–20), sell them into slavery (Isa 50:1), and declare them no longer God's people (Hos 1:9). It is

16. See Levenson, 7, 13, 37.
17. Levenson, 19.

likely in this spirit, a covenant spirit, that Jesus turned away from his consanguineous mother and siblings and declared instead, "Whoever does the will of God is my brother and sister and mother" (Mark 3:31–35). Jesus's primary family, in this sense, is composed not of those who share his genetic makeup but of those who share his obedient spirit.[18]

At the same time, such remarks must be kept in tension with an underlying unconditional quality about covenant. Though Israel (and later the church) repeatedly fails and betrays its Lord in what the prophets portray as adulterous liaisons with other gods, Yahweh shows a determination to never give up or turn God's back on his people. The romance between God and his people is stormy and too often ruptures. But, as Jewish theologian Jon Levenson puts it in his beautiful and unparalleled treatment of covenant, God's "ardent passion for Israel . . . prevents that separation from ever becoming amicable, or, more important, permanent. . . . The sheer gratuity of God's establishment of covenant with Israel—the fact that the existence of covenant in the first place is a gift, not a reward—portends that it will survive Israel's malfeasance." So "to the extent that the covenant depends on the human partners' meeting its conditions, covenant is exceedingly fragile. To the extent that it depends on God's reliability, it is rock-solid."[19]

Thus we may speak of God's commitment to Israel (and later to the church) as unconditional. God initiates and stays with covenant even as the covenant people falter. God will keep loving no matter what. "But graciousness does not mean normlessness, and if love is to be a relationship and not just an ephemeral and episodic

---

18. On the connection between obedience and biblical covenant, see Hoskyns and Davey, *Crucifixion-Resurrection*. See also deSilva, *Honor, Patronage*, 202–6.

19. Levenson, *Love of God*, 114, 115–16, 121.

sentiment, it must impose norms of its own (even if violating them does not terminate the relationship)."[20]

Compare again human parents and children. Parents can love unconditionally, never withdrawing their final and ongoing commitment to their children. But especially in relation to younger children, parents do know what is best mediately and in the long term, and not just immediately. Thus loving parents, not least unconditionally loving parents, do harbor moral expectations and make stipulations—and yes, on occasion, even commands—to their children. At their best and in all circumstances, what such parents hope for is the eventual and enduring flourishing, if not the immediate appeasement, of their children.

Similarly, God's covenant love is unconditional. But it aims to sustain a substantial and long-term relationship, so it includes what might be considered "conditional" elements. As Levenson says, "It is unconditional in that the love comes into, and remains, in force even when nothing has been done to deserve it. . . . But the relationship is also conditional in that it involves expectations and stipulations, and suffers and turns sour if they are not met."[21]

Covenant, and the fidelity it enacts, may be contrasted with neoliberal contractualism.[22]

Contract is the fundamental basis of the neoliberal economy (and of a liberal economy more generally). A contract is a punctual agreement enacted between two parties, for a set period, and under specified conditions. Contracts, and contracting parties, are calculating

---

20. Levenson, 54.

21. Levenson, 62.

22. For theological, covenantal reflections on the limits and shortcomings of liberal contractualism, see Campbell, *Pauline Dogmatics*, 211–15; and *Deliverance of God*, 301–9.

and careful. Their trust and fidelity, such as they are, intend to serve the immediate interests of the contracting parties—and do not extend beyond the terms of the contract. In other words, the relationships they establish are limited and completely conditional.

Though Christians certainly participate in this contractual economy, it is not their ultimate economy. The church as first family is the *oikos* grounded in God's encompassing economy. It works most fundamentally by way of covenant rather than contract. It is about establishing and maintaining deep, full, thoroughly faithful, long-term, and open-ended relationships.

Of course, the ultimate covenant is that between God and his people. Yahweh is "the faithful God who maintains covenant loyalty" (Deut 7:9). God's faithfulness extends "to the clouds"; it is "steadfast love" in practice (Ps 36:5; see also Ps 89). Prophets such as Hosea and Ezekiel use faithful marriage as a picture of God's enduring, determined commitment to the chosen people, God's bride. This is picked up in the New Testament, as at Ephesians 5:31–32, and in Revelation, which sees the church and the renewed creation as Christ's bride.

Note well that this covenant fidelity of Yahweh represents a particular kind of divinity. The Greek gods, after all, put no premium on fidelity to their people. Pagan divinity in general is not so much to be trusted as outwitted and manipulated. But fidelity is a key mark of the God revealed to Israel and the church—the God who chose, finally, to answer human betrayal with the cross rather than a flood of destruction. And so if we are to live in the light of this, the true divinity, we must strive to become the kind of people who practice at least enough covenant faithfulness to know what it looks like. Christians live lives of fidelity in order to become people who can learn to recognize the God of enduring faithfulness, the God of Israel and Jesus Christ.

Marriage then becomes a central practice and test case of undergoing and learning covenant faithfulness. In covenantal marriage, two people promise each other, the church, and God that they will be faithful to each other until death, whether or not what intervenes is poverty or riches, sickness or health. Thus covenant is risky and admits no qualifications or reservations.

Neoliberal contractualism is hemmed about by qualifications; its form of marriage is enamored of contractual arrangements such as no-fault divorce and prenuptial agreements. Whereas covenantal marriage aims at a union of selves, contractualism aims only at a union of interests. It promises faithfulness only so long as one (or both) parties do not find a "better" option. It hedges its bets and is based on careful and ongoing calculation. For neoliberalism, with contractualism and competition at its roots, enduring trust is decidedly not a premium. And what is true here of neoliberal marriage is true of its wider economy: the "suzerains" that are neoliberal employers owe no fidelity to their workers or "vassals," who are fungible and disposable.

Neoliberal capitalism inhibits the Christian practice of marriage and family because the market has overrun its boundaries. We face a belligerent bottom line that invades all aspects or spheres of our existence. We are coached to see not just the bartering of bread and soap but the whole of our lives in the ways of the market. We too easily fall into neoliberal economistic language that reconceives family practices and relationships. We speak of children presenting "time demands." Spouses should "invest" in one another to "promote" intimacy, or their marriage may become "unproductive."

So doing, we slip into the conceptuality of Milton Friedman, Gary Becker, and their compatriots in the Chicago school of economics, who tell us marriage is not so much about love and bearing witness to the fidelity of Yahweh as about supply and demand for spouses, that a man commits suicide when "the total discounted lifetime utility remaining to him reaches zero," and that we should address the shortage of infants for adoption by quoting baby prices like soybean futures.[23]

By contrast, the covenantal economy of the church's *oikos* shapes us not as free-floating entrepreneurs of the self but as whole-orbed persons who live in long-term relationships with God and one another. These relationships are not calculating but committed. They are between people who need and depend on one another, who are each and every one uniquely important—not fungible or interchangeable with other people like standardized machine parts. They aim at a union of selves, not merely of interests. All told, they embody fidelity and witness to a creator-redeemer God of unfailing faithfulness and steadfast love.

COVENANT AND SAME-SEX RELATIONSHIPS

Apocalyptic and covenant suggest fresh angles on a pressing concern of today's church and world: same-sex, sexually active relationships.

We have seen how the apocalyptic coming of Jesus Christ removes marriage as an obligation and elevates the status of singleness. This is the case because the old world or age has passed away in Christ's apocalypse, and another—new creation!—has been born. With Jack in Emma Donoghue's *Room*, we must now declare, "Everything is new." In the strong terms of J. Louis Martyn, distinctions "once so crucial, no longer matter. . . . One knows the old world to have died, because . . . its fundamental structures are gone."[24] In Paul's words, perhaps drawn from a baptismal liturgy

23. See Wolfe, *Whose Keeper?*, 31–32, 38.
24. Martyn, "Apocalyptic Antinomies," 117–18.

that predated him, "There is no longer Jew or Greek, there is no longer slave or free, there is no longer male and female" (Gal 3:28).

As we saw earlier, no biblical distinction was more fundamental than the one between Jew and Gentile. Slave or free, meanwhile, was a binary of profound force and separating distinction, with slaves believed to be almost naturally consigned to their lesser status. For Paul to say further that the absolute, binary distinction between male and female was eliminated hardly needs further comment: this is still a binary our contemporary world leans on with great emphasis.

If such basic binaries were apocalyptically undercut, we may fairly wonder what this means for the status of the binary—which some take to be no less natural and little less fundamental—between heterosexuality and homosexuality. At the least, it surely means that a specific sexual orientation is less fundamental and less significant than identity and unity in Christ. More, it can push us to reevaluate same-sex relationships and their acceptability in our place and time.

Some faithful Christian scholars take to heart the apocalyptic breaking down of barriers between clean and unclean food and extend it to contacts with human flesh. "If the earth and all that is in it belongs to the Lord, . . . as the twenty-fourth Psalm says (Paul quotes it in the Corinthian correspondence), then its contents cannot, in principle, be divided into clean and unclean things," Paul Griffiths writes. "And this must go not only for food, but for anything with which human flesh might come into contact."[25] This includes what Griffiths calls "cleavings" with flesh of the same sex.

Some cleavings and their "caresses" are inherently violent—such as that of an adult with a child—and are to be abhorred. But others, such as the cleavings and caresses between two same-sex adults

25. Griffiths, *Christian Flesh*, 72.

who are committed to each other's welfare, are not. "Copulative caresses" have two principal goods: they can produce offspring, and they can profoundly unite and bind together the lives of the couple involved in the caressing. Though the first good is not available to a same-sex relationship, the second is.

The unitive, generative good is honored in heterosexual relationships where one or both of those cleaving are infertile or, as with age, beyond fertility. It is also generally honored among the many Christians who practice birth control. Griffiths argues that faithful but nonprocreative sexual acts should not be seen as merely a "damaged, inadequate, and deceptive form of copulation." Sex includes procreation but signals and involves more than it. So it should perhaps not be denied to Christians who would embody and enact it within committed, ongoing same-sex relationships and so know the profound unitive, generative good of sexual expression.[26]

This line of reasoning is bolstered by remembering that it is only since the late nineteenth century that sexual orientation, a deep-set affinity and disposition toward one sex or the other, began to be generally recognized. The same-sex genital contact of Paul's place and time—which he clearly condemns—was of a decidedly different phenomenology than the modern cast of same-sexual orientation. In the Roman Empire, same-sex pederasty was acceptable, and slaves (children as well as adults) were considered the sexual property of their masters, to be exploited as the master wished. Members of the ruling Julio-Claudian dynasty, which Paul may have in mind as he lists grievous Gentile sins in Romans 1, famously debauched and sexually exploited. Caligula boasted of incest with

26. Griffiths, 138–45, quotation at 143. See as well Tonstad, *Queer Theology*, 35–42. This is also the crux of a much-acclaimed essay by Rowan Williams, "The Body's Grace."

his sisters, had homosexual liaisons, and was a known rapist (once assaulting a bride on her wedding day). Nero raped his younger brother and later had him murdered and was notorious for orgiastic parties replete with heterosexual and homosexual acts.[27] In short, the "homosexuality" Paul observed was episodic, exploitative, and inherently violent. It was not a matter of a stable, loving, ongoing relationship between two adults of the same sex.

The case for the viability of Christianly acceptable same-sex relationships is only strengthened further in light of our consideration of covenant and its deep theological meaning. Covenant, we have seen, is a means of witnessing to the fidelity of God to his people and, indeed, to all of creation. It is committed rather than calculating and aims at a union of selves rather than interests. As such, it in no way bars two same-sex partners. They may as effectively embody and witness to God's covenantal self and being as two united heterosexuals.

Douglas Campbell neatly summarizes,

A covenantal account of a marriage is clearly not as interested in the form or structure of the marriage—whether it is procreative and/or gendered—as it is in the relational tenor of the marriage. Is it a covenant? Are the adults pledged unconditionally and faithfully to one another in perpetuity? Do they love one another and commit to one another in this way, thereby reflecting the relational dynamics of the Trinity? If so, it seems fair to recognize that they can marry, which seems to lead fairly quickly to the conclusion that

---

27. Keesmaat and Walsh, *Romans Disarmed*, 333n19, 335–36.

nonnormative populations can marry, in addition to the majority heterosexual population.[28]

APOCALYPSE AND BASELINE COMMUNISM

For all its talk about freedom and comprehensiveness, the neoliberal capitalistic market occludes significant economic dimensions and practices. In the long view of human history, the neoliberal market is unique in its claim for an economy that stands apart and insulated from communal morality and spirituality. The ancients, for example, saw the economy as nested within a moral frame—the means of the economy were meant to serve ethically determined ends. Of course, we should not romanticize this *oikonomia*, for it was "generated by slave labor and the denial of citizen rights to women."[29] But it reminds us that our wisest, oldest philosophers sought to interpret and enact economy in light of morality.

Furthermore, the church through its history has tried to practice economy in an ethical context. Stipulations concerning usury, for example, run well into the modern period (and some usury laws, however defanged, are still on the books). Christian socialism, which calls the market to moral account, has a venerable if checkered history, though it is too easily and too often simply neglected.[30] Even Christian accounts quite friendly to capitalism usually break

---

28. Campbell, *Pauline Dogmatics*, 635. See also the nuanced affirmative case, distinguishing between "marriage" and "non-procreative covenant relationships," in Song, *Covenant and Calling*.

29. Leshem, "What Did the Ancient Greeks?"

30. Typical contemporary accounts of socialism, such as Sunkara's *Socialist Manifesto*, often entirely ignore Christian socialism. For a significant and compendious exception, see Dorrien, *Social Democracy*.

neoliberal rules and seek to have capitalism answer to certain extra-market moral norms or demands.[31]

At a basic level, the market qua market exhibits moral idiocy. This can be confirmed by a walk through the common drugstore. Cigarettes are stocked adjacent to smoking-cessation aids. Diet and weight-loss concoctions sit next to high-calorie snacks and sugar-loaded beverages. Fertility pills are down the aisle from contra-ceptives. In actual practice, no sane consumer can be or is guided simply and solely by the market.

Speaking at an equally basic level, every minimally working human economy has a strong, underlying communistic dimension. At first blush, this may sound shocking and revolting. But think not of state-directed and state-compulsory communism, as in the Soviet Union and China, which are indeed revolting. Think instead of consanguineous family, where all goods are shared in common. Think of close friendships or tightly knit neighborhoods, where snowblowers and mowers and tools are freely passed back and forth, or a hand is lent with moving house or barn building. Think of bystanders rushing to help a child who has fallen onto subway tracks. Think of the aftermath of natural disasters such as storms, fires, blackouts, or an economic collapse, where each gives of their ability to each according to their needs.[32] Then, often if not always, people resort to a "rough-and-ready communism."[33]

Think too not just about morality but about common pleasures. As David Graeber puts it, "Solitary pleasures will always exist,

---

31. See, for example, Waters, *Just Capitalism*. See also Ahn, *Just Debt*. Working within a capitalist framework, Ahn draws on Islamic, Jewish, and Christian ethics to propose a more just conception and management of debt.

32. For an exploration of postdisaster communism, see Solnit, *Paradise Built in Hell*.

33. Graeber, *Debt*, 96.

but for most human beings, the most pleasurable activities almost always involve sharing something: music, food, liquor, drugs, gossip, drama, beds. There is a certain communism of the senses at the root of most things we consider fun."[34]

All this is because we are always already social creatures. For Christians, who believe all people are created by one God, fallen in one man (Adam), redeemed through one Savior, and destined for one new heaven and new earth, this claim should come as no surprise. With a theological overflow, we can agree with Graeber: "Baseline communism might be considered the raw material of sociality, a recognition of our ultimate interdependence that is the ultimate substance of social peace."[35]

Think again—and this time of the postapocalyptic believers and the new first family called church. In the immediate wake of Jesus's life, death, and resurrection, "All who believed were together and had all things in common; they would sell their possessions and goods and distribute the proceeds to all, as any had need" (Acts 2:44–45). And, "Now the whole group of those who believed were of one heart and soul, and no one claimed private ownership of any possessions, but everything they owned was held in common. With great power the apostles gave their testimony to the resurrection of the Lord Jesus, and great grace was upon them all. There was not a needy person among them, for as many as owned lands or houses sold them and brought the proceeds of what was sold. They laid it at the apostles' feet, and it was distributed to each as any had need" (Acts 4:32–35).

"Simply said," David Bentley Hart observes, "the earliest Christians were communists . . . , not as an accident of history but as an

34. Graeber, 99.
35. Graeber, 99.

imperative of faith." And if time and circumstances meant that not all subsequent Christians evinced communism as fully and intensely as the earliest, a call toward a vision of service to the common good echoed through the patristic period, founded on a truth taught by Basil the Great, Gregory of Nyssa, Ambrose of Milan, and John Chrysostom: "The goods of creation belong equally to all, and that immense private wealth is theft—bread stolen from the hungry, clothing stolen from the naked, money stolen from the destitute."[36]

Nor did such hopes, dreams, and practices cease with the patristic age. We can think of monasticism and mendicancy as well as such present-day movements as the Catholic Workers, the Bruderhof, and the (usually Protestant) New Monastics.[37] Such "purist" movements have great value and pertinence, as does the less "purist" yet still significant giving in face of need—serving at soup kitchens and homeless shelters, donating cars and groceries—that happens day to day and week to week in ordinary urban, suburban, and rural churches.

The apocalypse, as I said in chapter 3, brings a moment of crisis and judgment. Jesus is revealed to be Lord of creation and history. We are confronted with the decision of whether to accept and acknowledge this. Apocalypse is not something that emerges progressively or naturally and inherently but is a sudden and once-for-all invasion.[38] In consequence, "the Body of Christ is not an option to be set alongside other equally plausible alternatives. It is not a private ethos or an elective affinity. It is not a call to withdrawal, but to revolution. It truly enters history as a *final* judgment that has

---

36. Hart, "What Lies beyond Capitalism?," 36 and 38.

37. For a discussion of monasticism, old and new, as an ongoing renewal movement and "event" within the church, see my "Monkhood of All Believers."

38. As Hart affirms; "What Lies beyond Capitalism?," 38.

nevertheless already been passed; it is inseparable from the extraordinary claim that Jesus is Lord over all things."[39] If we profess that Jesus is Lord, we cannot get around the clearly nonacquisitive and poverty-resisting ethic taught and practiced by him and his people, Israel.[40] We may even go so far as Stanley Hauerwas and recognize that "being wealthy is a disability for anyone who desires to be a Christian."[41] Jesus, in a statement that was hardly an outlier, said as much plainly: "It is easier for a camel to go through the eye of a needle than for someone who is rich to enter the kingdom of God" (Mark 10:25; see also Matt 19:24; Luke 18:25).

In light of the apocalypse, the church can at least be honest about the shortcomings of neoliberal capitalism. As Hart writes, "It eventuates in a culture of consumerism, because it must cultivate a social habit of consumption extravagantly in excess of mere natural need or even (arguably) natural want. It is not enough to satisfy natural desires; a capitalist culture must ceaselessly seek to fabricate new desires, through appeals to what 1 John calls 'the lust of the eyes.'" Furthermore, "A capitalist society not only tolerates, but positively requires, the existence of a pauper class, not only as a reserve of labor value, but also because capitalism relies on a stable credit economy, and a credit economy requires a certain perennial supply of perennial debtors. . . . The perpetual insolvency of the working poor and lower middle class is an inexhaustible font of profits for the institutions upon which the investment class depends."[42]

39. Hart, 37.
40. For a deft summary of nonacquisitiveness and concern for the poor as undeniable and consistent biblical values, see Collins, *What Are Biblical Values?*, 171–211.
41. Hauerwas, "How Risky?," 47.
42. Hart, "What Lies beyond Capitalism?," 33–34.

By its "purist" movements, the church witnesses perhaps most robustly to another economy. By the less purist but still significant communist acts of "ordinary" churches, it also stands as a kind of contrast economy to that of neoliberal capitalism. Otherwise, it confronts the neoliberal economy by critically engaging it at strategic points and working with national and international governmental bodies on moves it considers more proximately just and fair to all people, not least the precariat—and indeed, all creation. (See more on this in chapter 5.)

NEW CREATION AND THE ECONOMY OF GOD

In an explicitly apocalyptic passage, the apostle Paul writes, "So with us; while we were minors, we were enslaved to the elemental spirits of the world. But when the fullness of time had come, God sent his Son, born of a woman, born under the law, in order to redeem those who were under the law, so that we might receive adoption as children" (Gal 4:3–5). Examining this text, J. Louis Martyn avers that "the elements of the world" (*ta stoicheia tou kosmou*) for the Galatians would have been understood as the traditional, undergirding, and constituting elements of the earth: water, air, and fire. "Specifically, they almost certainly heard of some form of the ubiquitous speculation about the elements that constitute the world's foundations."[43] And even these primary, basic elements (*stoicheia*) had been displaced and overthrown in Christ. No longer were the *stoicheia* to be worshiped or regarded as gods.

Demythologizing and analogizing this passage, we may wonder what may be regarded as *stoicheia* in the present day. I submit that

---

43. Martyn, "Christ and the Elements," 129. See also the extended discussion of the *stoicheia* in de Boer, "Cross and Cosmos."

few candidates serve as exactly as the neoliberal market, proposed as the pervasive and all-encompassing context for the proper and final workings of our world. This is captured in Paddy Chayefsky's script for the film *Network*, in which media mogul Arthur Jensen pontificates that now, "there are no nations, there are no peoples . . . there is only one holistic system of Systems . . . one interwoven, interacting system of currency which determines the totality of life on this planet. That is the natural order of things today. That is the atomic and subatomic and galactic structure of things today."[44] In its totality, in its naturalization, in its bid to provide "the atomic and subatomic and galactic structure of things today," neoliberalism is our contemporary instance of the *stoicheia*.

If so, it is also an instance of the *stoicheia* that have been displaced and overthrown in Christ. In another apocalyptic passage, Paul writes that at the cross, "[Christ] disarmed the rulers and authorities and made a public example of them, triumphing over them in it" (Col 2:15). Apocalyptically speaking, neoliberalism is named in and through the cross, unmasked and denaturalized as one of or the constituting element of the world and its ultimate workings. For through the cross, the great and truly ultimate *oikonomia* is seen to be not the untrammeled market but the economy of God.

At the conclusion of his Letter to the Galatians, Paul rhapsodizes, "May I never boast of anything except the cross of our Lord Jesus Christ, by which the world has been crucified to me, and I to the world. For neither circumcision nor uncircumcision is anything; but a new creation is everything!" (Gal 6:14–15). New creation has arrived, though it is not yet fully manifested. In it, the capacious economy of God has been revealed. Beside it, the neoliberal economy is puny and constricted. The market as a gigantic

44. As quoted in McCarraher, *Enchantments of Mammon*, 508.

information processor cannot and does not contain or process care for the weak and the "loser"—in a word, mercy—or care for creation or nature as a good in itself. It does not embrace community, covenant love, grace, or miracle. In the economy of God, all of these realities live. And they can thrive.

5

FREED FROM NATIONALISM, FREED FOR CATHOLICITY

From its genesis, neoliberalism has been politically concerned and active. The founding neoliberals recognized the necessity of state power to enact, undergird, and enforce an absorbing and all-encompassing market. Subsequent neoliberal think tanks lobbied governing bodies on behalf of the neoliberal vision. Politicians from Reagan and Thatcher onward worked to make the vision a functioning reality, refashioning and redirecting government accordingly. Neoliberalism does not spring out of thin air; it enlists and requires the strong action of strong states.

At the same time, the thoroughgoing individualism of liberalism and neoliberalism erodes traditional rationales for why the state deserves our commitment and obeisance. As an individual with weakened ties to family, territory, and history, why should I sacrifice my self-interest—let alone my life—for the good of a nation-state? Furthermore, neoliberal capital notoriously crosses national boundaries and seeks to establish a *global* market. Therefore, nationalism (loyalty to a particular nation-state) is repellent if not inimical to the cosmopolitan neoliberal mind. This is the face of "progressive neoliberalism" the critic Carl Raschke excoriates, finding it ensconced not least in our universities and culture industries.[1]

Still, no ideology, however hegemonic its aims, is gifted with a blank slate. So neoliberalism must, to a degree, make do with the world as it is. And it is a world composed of various nation-states. Needing government, neoliberalism must appeal to and seek to direct national governments. And needing the loyalty of peoples, neoliberalism must turn to something that evokes loyalty and resonates intensely in the breasts of actual human beings. That "something," in our world, is nationalism. Nationalism, as it were, fills the gaps that individualism and cosmopolitanism cannot. Without the gaps filled, neoliberalism's whole armature would collapse.

In light of these realities, neoliberals have recognized that nationalism of a sort is irreversible and ineradicable. Thinkers such as Friedrich Hayek and Ludwig von Mises prohibited any economic nationalism—capital and trade must be allowed to pass any and all national borders. But they allowed for what they sometimes called cultural nationalism. This form of nationalism would celebrate the culture of homelands and include the admiration and use of national flags, anthems, and coinage.[2] The nationalism we will be confronting in this chapter is a form of cultural nationalism—more specifically, white Christian American nationalism.

CHRISTIANIZED NATIONALISM AND ITS ERRANT HERMENEUTIC

Nationalism is a relative latecomer in history. Nation-states arose in the eighteenth century and became prevalent only in the nineteenth

1. Raschke, *Neoliberalism and Political Theology*.
2. Slobodian, *Globalists*, 93, 95, 98, 105, and 111.

century and following. Accordingly, nationalism first appeared in the eighteenth century.[3] Ironically, given that nationalism is now often most potently a right-wing phenomenon, nationalism originated as a leftist and revolutionary force following the French Revolution. "As a set of shared feelings," Davies writes, "nationalism began in the context of revolutionary, popular fervor, and was only much later adopted by traditionalists to prop up the political establishment."[4]

Nationalism has been entangled with religion—or has served more or less directly as a religion—from its beginnings. Early nationalisms were syncretized with the Bible. In 1719, Isaac Watts translated the Psalms, replacing the word *Israel* repeatedly with *Great Britain*.[5] Disillusioned English settlers in America aimed at creating the "true Israel of God" and considered themselves "God's peculiar people" led into the wilderness to expand and reform "England, God's Israel." The earliest known use of the English term *nationalism* was in the mid-nineteenth century, referring to the divine election of a nation (other than ancient Israel).[6]

In our time, a powerful distillation of this nationalism is found in Peter Marshall and David Manuel's *The Light and the Glory*, first published in 1977 and most recently in a revised and expanded edition in 2009. More than a million copies of the book have been sold, and it has been widely used in private Christian schools and Christian home schools.

Surveying American history from 1492 to 1793, Marshall and Manuel claim to see God's providential hand at work from the

3. See Cavanaugh, *Migrations of the Holy*, 11.
4. Davies, *Nervous States*, 141.
5. See the discussion in Jennings, *Christian Imagination*, 210–20.
6. Anderson, *Chosen Nation*, 42–43, 51n30.

founding of the nation, to various spectacular turns in memorable battles, and through Christian revival movements. Their tale is declensionist, seeing the present-day nation—marked by widespread abortion, the approval of same-sex marriage, and various natural disasters that signal God's judgment—in a moment of grave decline. The hope, as they understand it, is for a faithful remnant of Christians to stave off God's final judgment until the country as a whole returns robustly to its Christian roots.

Marshall and Manuel are clear that Israel's covenant relationship with God was not a unique, singular event but the first and exemplary instance of God's ongoing relating to the various nations of the world. For them, God chose America as he chose Israel—albeit at a different time and in a different place—to be a light to the nations, to establish a new promised land. The likes of William Bradford, John Winthrop, and George Washington are the new Moseses for the new Israel. As Marshall and Manuel straightforwardly put it, in America, "God was making His most significant attempt since ancient Israel to create a new Israel of people living in obedience to the laws of God, through faith in Jesus Christ."[7]

The authors are explicit about their hermeneutic for arriving at such a reading of American history. Hearkening to the Pilgrims and Puritans, they read the Bible typologically:

This meant that they saw "types" of New Testament events or persons in the Old Testament. In this practice they were in good company. Even the New Testament writers themselves understood the Israelites' crossing of the Red Sea as a prefiguring of the sacrament of Baptism in the New Testament,

7. Marshall and Manuel, *Light and the Glory*, 20.

and the Israelites' forty years in the desert as a prefiguring or type of Jesus's forty days in the wilderness.

America's early Christian settlers, then, used typology to interpret God's dealings in their own lives. They felt that certain passages in the Bible, originally addressed to Israel, also applied to them.[8]

The problem here is not typology. New Testament authors and subsequent preachers and writers in the Christian tradition indeed employ it (see, for example, 1 Cor 10:1–13). The problem instead is an employment of typology that violates and distorts the original types. Paul and other New Testament writers do not envision ancient Israel as one "attempt" among others to come for God to establish a chosen people. In this regard, Israel is singular and unique: *the* chosen people. The (Gentile) church, inasmuch as it partakes of Israel's unique identity, is but an extension of the irreplaceable Israel, a "wild olive shoot" grafted into the "rich root" of the unrepeatable original tree (Rom 11:17). And the New Testament writers always address the church, and *never* the Roman state (or any other state), as the people of God in Jesus Christ.

William Cavanaugh pinpoints the issue with the disastrous hermeneutic employed by the likes of Marshall and Manuel: "The problem, in my view, is that the political presence of the biblical God is mediated through the official discourse of America and not through a distinctively Christian body that stands under the explicit authority of Jesus Christ. The church as mediator between God and America—a church that has the critical distance to pronounce judgment as well as blessing—is in danger of being erased. What has happened in effect is that America has become the new

8. Marshall and Manuel, 20.

church." Against American exceptionalism, Cavanaugh argues, "God has elected Israel, and not any nation-state, to be the primary agent of God's activity in history." Furthermore, "in the Christian theological tradition, the fulfillment of Israel is not any nation-state, but the church." And even then, Israel's uniqueness and irreplaceability stand: "Paul does not believe that Israel had been cast off or replaced by the church. . . . The church is to remain open to Israel, for the eschatological goal is the gathering of the whole of Israel. The nonbelieving Jews are not rejected (Rom. 11:1), but will once again be restored to Israel (Rom. 11:26–27)."[9]

To appreciate the dimensions of the problem, it is important to remember that the fallacious hermeneutic is not confined to Marshall and Manuel. Though they offer an especially pointed example of it, the confusion of America with Israel and/or the church rings down through history and into the present day. In *Uncle Tom's Cabin* (1852), Harriet Beecher Stowe saw the United States as the base of salvation for the whole world: "Thus, the [American] Christian family and Christian neighborhood would become the grand ministry as they

---

9. Cavanaugh, *Migrations of the Holy*, 104, 105, 106. Cavanaugh further complexifies the picture by observing that the biblical Israel was not a nation-state in any modern sense. Over the course of the Old Testament and into the New, Israel was a tribal confederation, then later a Temple community and a federation of synagogues. Its experience "of what might be called statehood was relatively brief, between David and the conquests by the Assyrians and Babylonians" (105). Pertinently, Jewish theologian Jon Levenson writes, "In covenant theology, Sinai serves as an eternal rebuke to man's arrogant belief that he can govern himself. The state is not coeval with God. Rather, it was born at a particular moment in history and under the judgment of a disappointed God. In a better world, one in which man turns to God with all his heart, it would not exist. . . . For the theological tradition maintained that Israel had been a people before she was a worldly kingdom, a people to whom laws and even a destiny had already been given. She owes neither to the state" (cited in Anderson, *Chosen Nation*, 111).

were designed to be, in training our whole race for heaven." Later, Albert Beveridge, who served as the US Senator of Indiana from 1899 to 1911, thought America had a duty to bring Christianity and civilization to "savage and senile peoples." Woodrow Wilson considered the United States as situated and equipped to bring about the "ultimate peace of the world." Ronald Reagan announced, "I have always believed that this anointed land was set apart in an uncommon way, that a divine plan placed this great continent here between two oceans to be found by people from every corner of the earth who have a special love of faith and freedom." Bill Clinton called the United States the "indispensable nation." And George W. Bush described American ideals as "the hope of all mankind" that "shines in the darkness" and paraphrased a hymn to Jesus's life-giving blood by ascribing "power—wonder-working power" to the "goodness and idealism and faith of the American people."[10]

Political scientist Benjamin Lynerd has recently provided a masterful account of this "republican theology." Here *republican* is not simply to be identified with the GOP, though professions of American civil religion are now primarily concentrated there, especially among the white evangelicals who comprise such an important bloc of the party. Rather, Lynerd's republican theology focuses on the merger of America as the chosen nation with the Lockean social contract and free-market values. Republican theologians "transpose the evangelical conversion narrative to the national level and envision the spread of democracy as linked to the spread of the gospel." Interestingly and importantly, African American Christians are less fervent adherents of American civil religion. "While freedom from slavery became an animating theme of black religion in the nineteenth century," writes

10. Quotations cited in LaMothe, *Care of Souls*, 139–40; and Dean, *For the Life*, 189n179.

Lynerd, "the Lockean philosophy of limited government never did. Neither did slaves and freemen buy into the idea that America was a chosen nation by virtue of its republicanism and its Christianity."[11]

LITURGIES, WAR, AND APOCALYPTIC

Nationalism operates as a functional if not declared religion. It parodies and substitutes the nation-state for the church. Other religious dimensions are clear in its pervasive use of patriotic cultural liturgies, or public and identity-constituting ceremonies.[12] July 4 stands as American nationalism's high holy day. Liturgies including parades and speeches (sermons) are vital. "Saints" such as the Founding Fathers and Abraham Lincoln are memorialized and venerated. The flag is prominent and treated as a sacred symbol. Fireworks evoke wars crucial to the nation's founding and survival.

But nationalism's liturgies extend beyond a single day on the calendar. The Pledge of Allegiance is regularly recited in schools. Francis Bellamy, the author of the pledge, explicitly meant it to be an ethos- and character-shaping ritual, sinking deeply and formatively into the imagination of schoolchildren. He commented, "It is the same way with the catechism, or the Lord's Prayer."[13]

Nationalistic liturgies also permeate sporting events. Professional football especially is marked by mandatory singings of the

11. Lynerd, *Republican Theology*, 42 and 127. For data on the prevalence and intensity of Christian nationalism in today's United States, see Whitehead and Perry, *Taking America Back for God*. For a meticulous account of patriarchical, militaristic Christian nationalism in white evangelicalism across the past seventy-five years, see Du Mez, *Jesus and John Wayne*.

12. On "secular" liturgies that perfuse society and shape ethos and character, see Smith's Cultural Liturgies trilogy, particularly volume 1, *Desiring the Kingdom*.

13. Cavanaugh, *Migrations of the Holy*, 119.

national anthem and spectacular halftime events that feature the flag and lionize soldiers.[14] The presence of soldiers points to a significant element of American nationalism: its militarism.

As the early twentieth-century cultural critic Randolph Bourne memorably remarked, "War is the health of the State."[15] Nothing unites the atomized citizens of liberal and neoliberal states like war. Soldiers give themselves for a higher cause, while citizens back home may forgo some degree of comfort on behalf of the "war effort." The usually disconnected, competing, and even hostile individuals coalesce against a common enemy.

As theologian Braden Anderson remarks, "Lacing [together] shared ends, the modern state must be defined by its mean, which is its supposed monopoly on the legitimate use of force. Thus war becomes 'the primary mechanism for achieving social integration in a society with no shared ends.' Violence is the state's *religio*, its habitual discipline for binding us to one another."[16] And the extreme stakes of war—life and death for individuals and the survival, or at least the welfare, of the country as a whole—lend themselves toward an almost irresistible temptation to conceive of the conflict in ultimate, religious terms.

Accordingly, we commonly say that in war, we "sacrifice" our sons and daughters. Taken at all seriously, this amounts to child sacrifice—a practice common to some ancient religions but considered outmoded in modern civilization. Discomforting as talk of child sacrifice may be, we do not usually admit another religious aspect of our wars. For no nation sets out to lose a war, to simply sacrifice its children. Wars are fought to be won. The point is not

14. For a telling novelistic explication of such events, see Fountain, *Billy Lynn's*.
15. Bourne, "State," 71.
16. Anderson, *Chosen Nation*, 18 (interior quote from William Cavanaugh).

to die but to kill. To that end, our soldiers are commissioned with priestly power: the power to purify the world of our enemies. In short, soldiers are preeminently not to *be* sacrificed but, like priests, to *enact* or *commit* sacrifice—the sacrifice of the enemy other. We thrust upon our soldiers the godlike power to kill, to decide who lives and who dies.

War, then, is an attempt at grasping control. Through war and other means, American nationalism sees America taking the reins of history and driving it toward its rightful end. Cavanaugh writes, "As Secretary of State Madeleine Albright said, 'We have our own duty to be authors of history.' . . . America is not simply subject to history but is charged with making history come out right." The United States thus claims godlike powers, including omniscience and omnipotence. "This aspiration is expressed in the Pentagon code names for two recent military operations, 'Infinite Reach' and 'Infinite Justice.' As General Tommy Franks has said, the new technology gives U.S. military commanders 'the kind of Olympian perspective that Homer had given his gods.' The aspiration of America in its position as exception to the nations is to rise above history, to see and act as God sees and acts." Thus in light of Christian orthodoxy, nationalism as religion presents an even greater threat than parodying the church: it posits a messiah and a god that are alternative to Jesus Christ and the God of Israel. "The deepest theological danger inherent in American exceptionalism . . . is that of the messiah nation that does not simply seek to follow God's will, but acts as a kind of substitute god on the stage of history. When the concept of chosenness becomes unmediated by the church and unmoored from the biblical narrative, the danger is that the nation will not only be substitute church but substitute god."[17]

17. Cavanaugh, *Migrations of the Holy*, 94–95, 96.

From an orthodox Christian, apocalyptic perspective, such a project is wildly off base and ill conceived. Apocalyptic means that history is not under the control of any nation-state but in the hands of the God of Israel. And as we observed in chapter 3, the Christian apocalyptic depends on God's initiation and acting, preeminently in the life, death, and resurrection of Jesus Christ. Accordingly, the church does not strive to save the world—God has done that in Christ, and we look ahead to the (apocalyptic) renewal of creation in Christ. So the church labors instead in the Spirit to witness to what God has done and will do through Christ. Remembering that *resurrection* is always a part of apocalyptic language, we see that "the resurrection opens up a new way of inhabiting the world for the new creation people who have been called into existence through the life, death, and resurrection of Jesus Christ. Freed from the oppressive need to constitute their own identity and secure their own existence, the life of this new creation people is characterized by gratitude and joy."[18] And it is characterized by living out of control and disavowing massive, violent attempts to make history come out right.

THE INEVITABILITY OF POWER AND POLITICS

But if the church does not arrogate to itself the aim of making history come out right, that does not mean it refuses all attempts to make changes in itself and in the world. The church hopes to be effectual in its witness. This is another way of saying that the church does not eschew all forms of power. For power does not necessarily corrupt, though absolute power may well corrupt absolutely. Put differently again, the church is and has a politics.

18. Dean, *For the Life*, 217–18.

When I once said as much to a Sunday school class, several members cringed. One stated, "That makes chills run up and down my spine." I think he reacted so because we are focused most often on national politics, often conducted forthrightly as a blood sport. We are accustomed to viciously partisan national politics and politicians who frequently show themselves to be power mongering, mendacious, and self-aggrandizing. That being so, we may want to think of the church as a sanctuary and a politics-free zone.

But power is inevitable in human life. Denying all occasions of power—of all abilities to effect or prevent change in our world—only drives the recognition of power underground, removes it from conscious consideration, and frees unconscionable holders of power to run rampant.[19] This is one reason church fights can be so bitter: those who have meager power to determine other spheres of their lives cling all the more desperately to the little congregational power they hold, which they often fail to name as power.

Instead, we must recognize that we are, as Aristotle said, political animals. Modern, Weberian conceptions of politics and power have too narrowly defined politics as the domain only of the state, which alone holds a monopoly on legitimate violence and the coercion it effects. This is sheerly a single kind of power: power over others used to dominate others.

But there are other sorts of power. There is power exercised *with* others and power exercised *for* others. Especially when we exercise power with others, we attempt to create a common form of life that serves the flourishing of all involved in the same project. As the theologian Luke Bretherton expresses it, "Given what it means to

19. For an excellent discussion of power from a theological and ecclesiological perspective, see Newson, *Radical Friendship*, 81–118.

be a fallen, finite, and frail creature whose survival and flourishing depend on the care of others, the formation of a common life is necessary to live. And the formation of any form of common life [of which the church is one] entails politics." Politics in this sense is "about forming, norming, and sustaining a common life between those who are the same and those who are different . . . , as configurations of power shape the conditions of life together at various scales from the local to the global." Politics is about "how to handle and distribute power constructively."[20]

Later Bretherton remarks that *politics* refers "to the relational practices through which a common world of meaning and action is created and cultivated."[21] His talk of "meaning" is helpful because it reminds us that action follows from the interpretation or construal of situations and circumstances. For instance, my interpretation of several people holding their hands in the air—and the appropriate action in response—depends on the situation or context of the hands up: whether in a bank, an African American church service, or a classroom. Happily, politics (especially of the politics-with sort) can often accommodate a number of different interpretations. Differing interpretations may enrich one another and at other times (partially or radically) correct one another. Thus it is rightly said that the church as a whole benefits from a variety of interpretations, expressions, or emphases: the Roman Catholic Church can remind us of the importance of unity, Anglicans of the significance of the incarnation, Pentecostals of the indispensability of the Holy Spirit's work, and so on.

It is in this vein that James K. A. Smith salubriously argues, "Hermeneutics is not a postlapsarian phenomenon, coming upon

20. Bretherton, *Christ and the Common Life*, 22 and 2, consecutively.
21. Bretherton, 34.

the scene after Eden. Instead interpretation is found already in Eden and is thus included in the pronouncement of goodness (Gen. 1:31). Hermeneutics, then, is not an evil to be overcome . . . but rather an aspect of creation and human life that ought to be affirmed as 'good.'" Interpretation is not only inevitable but commendable—an aspect of the beautiful, praiseworthy creation and not something plaguing us only after and because of the fall. "Plurality in interpretation is not the original sin; it is, on the contrary, the original goodness of creation: a creation where many flowers bloom and many voices are heard, where God is praised by a multitude from 'every tribe and language and people and nation' (Rev. 5:9), singing songs in a diversity of tongues, even worshiping through a diversity of theologies."[22]

What has this to do with politics? Simply that politics is a matter of differing interpretations and the negotiations between them. Politics in the broadest sense—including politics of power exercised for others and power exercised with others—like interpretation, is a "creational good, the goal of which is a just and loving common life, embodying as it does the good of association." In this sense, it is a prelapsarian (before the fall) good. But statecraft, "which entails the use of coercive, unilateral power, is a postlapsarian endeavor that at its best inhibits evil."[23]

Once again, an apocalyptic perspective has something to contribute. Striking an apocalyptic note, Bretherton writes, "Christ's

---

22. Smith, *Fall of Interpretation*, 19 and 32.

23. Bretherton, *Christ and the Common Life*, 25. Neither Bretherton nor I mean to imply that Christians can have nothing to do with statecraft. "Postlapsarian endeavors" may well include the vigorous service of Christians—just as physicians and nurses do honorable and often faith-motivated work, though disease and injury come after and because of the fall.

crucifixion, resurrection, and ascension reveal the impotence of fallen principalities and powers, who, when challenged, can only constrain, punish, and kill, and in doing so expose the limits of their power and their fear of their own limits. . . . By implication, at the most basic level of confession, Christians are to realize that the institutions and structures of this world, and those who rule them, while fearsome, are not in control, and do not have the last word." In its stories and tropes, "the Bible deconstructs and offers an alternative to *any* attempt to write a particular social, economic, and political order into the cosmic order in such a way that a contingent and fallen way of ordering time and space is inscribed with an immutable character and posited as inevitable, natural, or 'just the way things should be.'"[24] Hence principalities and powers such as neoliberalism and nationalism are unmasked, denaturalized, robbed of their bids for ultimacy and finality.

Nor is the apocalyptic merely negative. It does deny that humanity, nature, and history, *left only to their own devices*, are finally in control. But humanity, nature, and history are not left to their own devices. In Christ and through the Holy Spirit, something new and positive—God and God's economy—salutarily invades their realm. The new creation "is an irruption of the divine from outside human history, an act of grace that surpasses all that precedes it and changes the terms and conditions of the politics and social life that follow it."[25] Philosopher Michael Wyschogrod similarly argues that nature is not left solely to a godless evolutionism, but through the apocalyptic, it undergoes a "transformation that is discontinuous with nature as it has been. It envisages a break with the autonomy of nature brought about by God's intervention and not by working out the *telos* of

24. Bretherton, 20 and 22.
25. Bretherton, 239.

nature."[26] Relatedly, the Orthodox theologian John Zizioulas writes that the Holy Spirit brings the *eschata* (last things) into history: "He confronts the process of history with its consummation, with its transformation and transfiguration. By bringing the eschata into history, the Spirit does not vivify a pre-existing structure; He *creates* one; He changes linear historicity into a *presence*."[27]

Thus Bretherton insists that Christians, living in the time between the times, "do not have to establish regimes to control the time so as to determine the outcome of history. Rather, they can live without control because the resurrection and ascension of Jesus Christ already inaugurated the fulfillment of history, even as its consummation awaits Christ's return. . . . Christians are to cultivate forms of life in this age that bear witness to these eschatological possibilities even as they stand in solidarity with those still suffering." In doing so, the church looks to Jesus as a model of servant power: "To modern eyes, Jesus's ministry can look like a refusal of power. But it is better seen as a refusal of the spectacular but vacuous power that Satan offers [at the temptation in the wilderness]. It is also a refusal to exercise the unilateral, coercive power of institutionalized means of command and control (power over). But in refusing power over, Jesus affirms relational power (power with)."[28]

JUDICIOUSNESS AND THE AD HOC, PARTICULARITY, AND PATRIOTISM

Jesus's affirmation of relational power is consonant with biblical logic or grammar—that is, it fits in and crowns and clarifies the biblical

26. Bretherton, 129n34.

27. Zizioulas, *Being as Communion*, 180.

28. Bretherton, *Christ and the Common Life*, 136 and 132.

story and its overall depiction of the ways of God with the world. In *Does God Need the Church?* German theologian Gerhard Lohfink wonderfully encapsulates this grammar:

> How can anyone change the world and society at its roots without taking away freedom? It can only be that God begins in a small way, at one single place in the world. There must be a place, visible, tangible, where the salvation of the world can begin: that is, where the world becomes what it is supposed to be according to God's plan. Beginning at that place, the new thing can spread abroad, but only through persuasion, not through indoctrination, not through violence. Everyone must have an opportunity to come and see. All must have the chance to behold and test this new thing. Then, if they want to, they can allow themselves to be drawn into the history of salvation that God is creating. . . . What drives them to the new thing cannot be force, not even moral pressure, but only the fascination of a world that is changed.[29]

In theological terms, Lohfink is talking about the profoundly biblically derived doctrine of election. This doctrine is offensive to modern sensibilities. But correctly understood, it can be less offensive. Israel and the church do not exist as insular, hermetically sealed entities merely for their own thriving. They are elected for the sake of—for the very life of—the world. Phillip Cary summarizes it beautifully:

> In a more Jewish understanding of election, it is a good thing for the Gentiles that God has chosen the Jews as his own

29. Lohfink, *Does God Need the Church?*, 27.

people. For in the Bible, God always chooses some for the blessing of others. Abraham is chosen for the blessing of all nations, like his son Isaac and also his grandson Jacob, whose name is changed to Israel, the father of the chosen people. We would not be so offended by the biblical doctrine of election, I think, if we recognized that it has this structure: some are *chosen for the blessing of others.* . . . The structure of election is not God choosing some to the exclusion of others, but God choosing some *for the sake of* others. The key example of this for Christian theology, as Karl Barth realized, is Jesus Christ himself, the Jew who is God's beloved Son—his favorite son, we could well say—who is chosen to suffer for the redemption of the world. As the Jews are chosen to bless the nations, Christ is chosen to save the world. . . . What the doctrine of election really means is that God gave the Jewish people to the world because he intended all along to give us his own Son, the King of the Jews.[30]

The church is meant always and constantly to be engaged with the world. At its best, the church does so judiciously and on an ad hoc or case-by-case basis. We are not called to confront the world or culture globally or comprehensively, to decide once and for all to be for it, or against it, or in paradox with it, or to transform it.[31] Instead, we must engage particular instances or incarnations of culture. Some practices of culture we may indeed be against (white supremacy or pimping human bodies, for example). But others we may affirm and wholeheartedly participate in (such as medicine or

30. Cary, *Meaning of Protestant Theology*, 99–100. For another excellent meditation on election, see George Lindbeck's "The Gospel's Uniqueness."
31. Contra the usual readings of H. Richard Niebuhr's classic, *Christ and Culture.*

music).[32] Always we will bring a distinctive Christian twist or intonation, in the process often transforming culture in the light of Christ and his apocalyptic revelation. Always we will engage, and always we will return ever and again to the biblical witness of Israel and Christ for orientation in and with and for the world.

At our best, we do so with what might be called eschatological reserve. The kingdom has come, but we await its fullness. In the meantime, we see as through a glass, darkly (1 Cor 13:12) and in a piecemeal, fragmentary fashion. God's Spirit is not confined to the church; it has been poured out in and on the world (Joel 2:28; Acts 2:17–18). Other philosophies, religions, and ways of life may give us truths. The apostle Paul said to embrace all that is just, commendable, and of any excellence wherever it comes from (Phil 4:8–9). And we often cannot predict how other faiths or ways of life may press us to see new dimensions of the gospel.[33] So we need to be open, not behind fortress walls. Eventually, God will sort it all out, but in eschatological reserve, we let some apparent weeds grow with the wheat (Matt 13:24–30). We act as the historically constituted and situated creatures we are, often grasping the whole only foggily, if at all. But we are directed; we have various encounters and try, with Scripture's witness, to make sense of them. We pray and work for the kingdom come and coming, but we acknowledge that it has once come only through God's acts in Israel and Jesus Christ and will come in its fullness only through another act of God in Christ, the parousia.

Speaking in more technical language, the theologian Jason Springs reminds us that the story of Israel and Jesus Christ inculcates

32. I unpack this approach in detail in my *A Peculiar People*.
33. In this regard, it is interesting and telling how often social identities are initially named by outsiders. For instance, detractors were the first to use the designation "Christians" (Acts 11:26), and socialists first spoke of "capitalism."

in Jesus's followers an openness and hospitality to the stranger. The stranger is engaged on his or her own terms, so there will always be surprises, and the future will by no means be entirely predictable:

It is impossible to know antecedently what the form or occasion, or to what ends, Christians will need to engage non-Christians. The ad hoc and piecemeal character of the engagement with non-Christian viewpoints and claims permits casting into relief the world of discourse that is oriented around scriptural practices by both distancing and approximating that world of other linguistic domains. It permits redescribing (though not *reducing*) the scriptural in nonscriptural terms for ad hoc purposes. Barth, ever resisting systems, wrote, "After all, is it our job as Christians to accept or reject world-views? Have not Christians always been eclectic in their world-views—and this for very good reasons?"[34]

It is in this spirit of judiciousness that I have spoken critically of American history and nationalism. But in the same spirit, permit me here to speak affirmatively of so much that I approve of in the American experiment. I love the United States' stunning landscapes, from the plains to the mountains, from its redwood forests to its Gulf Stream waters, from sea to shining sea. I love its vast and variegated cities, especially Chicago, New York, and Los Angeles. The son of a farmer and rancher, I love people who dwell close to the soil. I love American stories and literature, not least Whitman and Dickinson, *Huckleberry Finn* and *Moby-Dick*, Toni Morrison and Cormac McCarthy. I love its endlessly inventive music, the glories of Louis Armstrong, Ma Rainey, Skip James, Blind Lemon Jefferson,

---

34. Springs, *Toward a Generous Orthodoxy*, 76.

Duke Ellington, John Coltrane, Aretha Franklin, Elvis, Hank Williams, Johnny Cash, Emmylou Harris, and so many more. I love that much of the American spirit is based in its Native American heritage, as with the majority of its state names—Oklahoma, Arkansas, Delaware, and so forth. I love that America has been a place where class does not always mean snootiness, assumed privilege, and radical social separation—so that my mother, the wife of a well-off farmer and school board president, could have as her best and lifelong friend a school janitor. I could go on, but this should be enough to make the point.[35]

The point, in short, is that though I firmly reject the messianic, militaristic nationalism sketched earlier, I do not disavow a judicious, chastened patriotism. For the Christian, such patriotism is secondary in terms of identity. Baptism and citizenship in heaven trump citizenship in the nation-state. The Nicene Creed is the Christian's ultimate pledge of allegiance. The cross and not the flag is the pre-eminent symbol of identification. The church is first family. God's economy is wider than deeper than the neoliberal economy.

The patriotism the Christian can avow is exactly analogous to what we owe our parents. We owe them particularly. A child's love and loyalty are demonstrated not when she admires motherhood in the abstract or in principle but when she embraces the one specific woman who gave her birth. So too, as George Orwell put it, patriotism is "devotion to a particular place and a particular way of life, one which one believes to be the best in the world but has no wish to force upon other people."[36] For me, my parents were and are the best parents in the world. But I am not aggressive or exclusive in this

---

35. For more on loving country judiciously but profoundly, see Pinches, *Gathering of Memories*.

36. Orwell, "Notes on Nationalism," 866.

claim. If you believe your parents are the best in the world, I can grant you that without dishonoring my parents. I have "no wish to force upon other people" the conviction that my mother is the greatest of all mothers. Likewise, a judicious patriotism freely allows and affirms the Brit's attachment to her country or a Mexican's to his.

Nor does my love of my parents force me to deny any of their shortcomings. You can disapprove of your father's divorce and yet have him remain your beloved father. You can regret and resist your mother's alcoholism and still claim her wholeheartedly as your mother. Likewise, says Randolph Bourne, "we are part of the country for better or worse. We have arrived in it through the operation of physiological laws, and not in any way through our own choice. By the time we have reached what are called the years of discretion, its influences have molded our habits, our values, our ways of thinking, so that however aware we may become, we never really lose the stamp of our civilization, or could become the child of another country."[37]

Such patriotism—as the very word itself suggests—operates on the same logic as that of love for parents. It is "essentially noncompetitive" and does not seek "competitive prestige" in that it allows citizens of other countries to be loyal patriots of their own homes.[38] It does not live or die by a succession of loyalty tests that endorse (or reject) its current government's latest actions. The patriot may disagree with or protest her country's actions without ceasing to be a patriot. In fact, we would not say that an adult child who passively stood by and let his parents undertake a destructive course of action was as loving as the one who actively worked to steer his parents off a disastrous path. The patriotism I am approving is critical and not blind or infantile. It is focused inward (toward one's country) and

37. Bourne, "State," 67–68.
38. Bourne, 68; Orwell, "Notes on Nationalism," 866.

not outward (in reaction to another country). It is "intensive and not belligerent" and ready to see one's nation alongside and cooperating with other nations.[39]

For Christian engagement with the world, then, patriotically and otherwise, the key word is *judiciousness*, and the methods are ad hoc. The engagement is often messy, constantly concerned with particulars, and always ongoing. It is open to the neighbor (and even the enemy), whom Christ calls us to love. Accordingly, the church's neighbor love "does not enter through abstract declarations of 'loving everyone' but starts by singling out the neighbor that appears alien to me, the neighbor whom I love in the midst of her obvious differences. It is with this neighbor that a more general love can start. This kind of neighbor love is intrusive and subversive to neoliberal ways of relating and being, as an individual must encounter her neighbor on the neighbor's own terms. To love this way is an affront to the exchange logic and value within neoliberalism because this kind of neighbor love makes no demand to reciprocate."[40]

And while we should remain highly critical of neoliberal capitalism, we may find surprising points of careful affirmation. The prophet Jeremiah surely regarded the Babylon that invaded his home and deported his people as inimical and odious. But he heard God tell him to counsel the Israelites to make Babylon their home and to "seek the welfare of the city where I have sent you into exile" (Jer 29:7). Similarly, writes Bretherton,

one can view Christianity and capitalism as ultimately antithetical to each other—capitalism being the latest iteration

39. Bourne, "State," 68. This and the previous two paragraphs draw on further elaborated material in my *Johnny Cash*, 123–26.
40. Day, *Religious Resistance to Neoliberalism*, 116–17.

of Babylon—while still seeing scope for ad hoc cooperation in the here and now to achieve penultimate goods. But
the plausibility of this approach depends on realizing that
capitalism is neither monolithic nor all-embracing. Capitalism is best conceived as a domineering power that takes
multiple forms, some better and some worse. Like Babylon,
capitalism is a symbol, structure, and culture of rule that
stands apocalyptically under judgment. . . . And yet, like all
forms of empire, alongside the decadent and the damned,
[capitalism] is capable of producing things of great scientific
merit and technological sophistication, as well as precious
artifacts of immense beauty.[41]

CATHOLICITY

"War," the comedian Jon Stewart quips, "is God's way of teaching Americans geography."[42] Stewart's comment points to how easy
it is for citizens of the nation-state—especially citizens of a globally powerful nation-state—to become insular and cut off from the
rest of the world. In short, the nation-state and nationalism can be
highly parochial.

But the church is catholic: universal and whole within each of
its parts. To understand this, we must turn to a central sacrament,
the Eucharist. At the Eucharist, Christians consume not just a part
of the ascended body of Christ but the whole. They are in turn
consumed by Christ and united to other Christians all around the
world (and even those Christians who are dead). Accordingly, "Each
eucharistic community is not merely a part of a whole, as if Christ

41. Bretherton, *Christ and the Common Life*, 352.
42. Quoted in Immerwahr, *How to Hide an Empire*, 171.

could be divided into parts, but a microcosm, a mini-cosmos in which the cosmic Christ is wholly present. . . . For this reason Paul can refer to the local assembly in Rome as *hole he ekklesia*, the whole church (Rom 16:23)."[43]

By this eucharistic means and medium, the church uniquely connects the part and the whole, the particular and the universal. As Cavanaugh puts it, "Eucharistic communities worldwide form one *Catholica* which, though universal, is always and only enacted at the local level. The global and the local are refracted in such a way that one becomes more united to the universal the more one is tied to the life of a particular local community."[44] Later elaborating, he explains, "The Eucharist gathers the many into one (cf. 1 Cor. 10.16–17) as an anticipation of the eschatological unity of all in Christ, but the local is not therefore simply subordinated to the universal." Instead, "each Eucharist performed in the local community makes present not part of Christ but the whole Christ, and the eschatological unity of all in Christ. . . . The Eucharist made it necessary to see the whole Christ in each local community, which at the same time united the communities, not through a single external centre or structure superimposed on the local, but through the presence of the whole Christ in each. The one Christ, then, is the centre of each Eucharistic community, yet the centre appears in many different places."[45] Accordingly, "in the first three centuries the term 'catholic Church' is most commonly used to identify the local church gathered around the Eucharist. Each particular church is not an administrative division of a larger whole, but is in itself a 'concentration' of the whole."[46]

43. Cavanaugh, *Being Consumed*, 71.
44. Cavanaugh, *Theopolitical Imagination*, 4–5.
45. Cavanaugh, 49 and 50.
46. Cavanaugh, 115.

Thus while state unity absorbs the local and particular into the universal, the church's eucharistic catholicity elides the antithesis between the local and the universal.[47] Consumers of the Eucharist are united to and in the whole Christ, participants in a transnational church, in which each community is at once networked to all others and yet never loses sight of its own particular location. Through eucharistic catholicity, the church transcends the parochialism of the nation-state and at the same time roots itself in real, living, concrete places.

Too often, the church lets that catholicity be overshadowed by the parochial nation-state. For instance, in the 2003 US invasion of Iraq, US churches almost entirely failed to reach out to and communicate with the church in Iraq. As a ramification of the invasion, the 1,400-year-old Iraqi church is now practically extinct. On the other hand, the sanctuary movement of the 1980s showed some awareness of catholicity, with US-based faith communities welcoming "illegal" immigrants from El Salvador and Nicaragua.

But failures at catholicity cannot be blamed solely on the nation-state. The church's own internal divisions prevent Christians from all sharing in the body and blood of Jesus Christ. Ecumenical relations, such as those among Lutherans and Anglicans and Roman Catholics, are crucial toward the end of all Christians sharing communion together.

There are other measures—stopgap but valuable—that can serve in the meantime. For example, the Ekklesia Project, a community of mainline Protestants, Roman Catholics, and free church Protestants, finds itself unable to participate in a common Eucharist at its annual gathering. Instead, and significantly, the project's gathering undertakes a foot-washing service, where (somewhat)

47. Anderson, *Chosen Nation*, 18.

separated kin still recognize one another as brothers and sisters in the first family called church.

In the end, however, there is no substitute for the full reclamation of catholicity—or at least, the fullest degree we can attain. The political philosopher Sheldon Wolin cannily recognizes the power of catholicity in the early, undivided church: "Whereas classical political thought ascribed a close, solidaristic nature to the political community, it had never conceived of it as a mystic body cohering around a godhead. But Christianity helped father the idea of a community as a non-rational, non-utilitarian body bound by a meta-rational faith, infused by a mysterious spirit taken into its members; a spirit that not only linked each participant with the center of Christ, but radiated holy ties knitting each member to his fellows. The Christian community was not so much an association as a fusion of spirits, a pneumatic being."[48]

Wolin notes that for Christians, "the church and not the city became *the vital medium for human improvement*, the symbol of human destiny."[49] To that should be added Cavanaugh's important observation: "What made the church different, however, was not only its choice an explicitly public and political term like *ekklesia*—as opposed to terms like *koinon* and *collegium* that designated [private and exclusive] associations—but its transgression of ordinary social boundaries to include women, men, children, slaves, Jews, Greeks, rich, and poor all within the same gathering."[50]

In these ways, the early church was not simply inclusive but catholic. And what it constituted, in the terms of its time, was very

---

48. Wolin, *Politics and Vision*, 119. For a rich theological unpacking of such "pneumatic being," see Zizioulas, *Being as Communion*.

49. Wolin, *Politics and Vision*, 157 (emphasis added).

50. Cavanaugh, *Field Hospital*, 20.

much a political body, a *politeuma*, which historian Mary Smallwood defines as "a recognized, formally constituted corporation of aliens enjoying the right of domicile in a foreign city and forming a separate, semi-autonomous civic body, a city within a city; it had its own constitution and administrated its internal affairs as an ethnic unit though official[ly] distinct from and independent of those of the host city." Dotan Leshem expands, "Seeing the society of believers as a politeuma in heaven is fundamental to patristic political thought. What singles out the Christian politeuma from the earthly ones is that it is subjected to Christ (and not Caesar), as . . . the savior . . . and master who holds the power to subject all things unto himself (Philippians 3:21)."[51]

As members of an alien but genuinely catholic *politeuma*, Christians recognized themselves to be pilgrims and wayfarers among earthly communities. Life as pilgrimage is a biblical theme, later developed most profoundly by Augustine, who wrote, "We are but travelers on a journey without a fixed abode; we are on our way, not yet in our native land; we are in a state of longing but not yet enjoyment."[52] Augustine's city of God awaited its ultimate and true home in the new heaven and the new earth. As Cavanaugh explains, "The city of God and the earthly city . . . correspond with the *already* and the *not yet* of salvation history. The city of God lives in recognition that Christ has already definitively triumphed over sin and evil. And yet not all have accepted this reality, and so the earthly city continues to mingle with the heavenly city until the final consummation of history." In this interpretation, "the two cities represent not material life and spiritual life but two different ways of dealing with the same world. . . . The

51. Leshem, *Origins of Neoliberalism*, 105. Smallwood is quoted here.
52. Augustine, *Confessions*, 150.

two cities similarly are best understood as two ways of using the same things, two different performances, one tragic and the other comic, that take place on the same stage."[53]

On this same earthly, worldly stage, both the church and the nation-state perform. They are not always at odds, but they are distinct from each other and have different ends or goals. The nation-state is inherently parochial. The church's catholicity embraces and roots itself throughout the whole world.

SOLIDARITY

Neoliberalism, with its individualism and thoroughgoing competition, has no place for the solidarity of humans with one another and with all of creation. Solidarity is a reality it at best ignores and at worst tears down.

The church's catholicity, however, embraces people from all nations and inclines the church toward solidarity not only with persons from all nations but with the entirety of creation. The antithesis between the "church" and the "world," which is certainly a Pauline and Johannine motif, here needs to be carefully understood. The "world," in these terms, should not be understood as synonymous with creation. Creation is triply sanctified in the Christian story: all has been created good; Christ's incarnation blesses all material, fleshly reality; and Christ's bodily resurrection and ascension take transformed physical creation into heaven, beside the very throne of God. Moreover, the cosmic order, in Paul's thought, is not sinful. It has been subjected to the futility of death through humanity's sinfulness, not its own, and is destined for apocalyptic liberation (Rom 5:12–21; 8:18–27).[54]

---

53. Cavanaugh, *Field Hospital*, 151 and 154.
54. Beker, *Paul the Apostle*, 222.

Thus the church/world distinction should never be confused with the church/creation distinction. Rather, the "world" (in a pejorative sense) "identifies everything *in* and outside the church that resists the mediation of Jesus and refuses to work 'with the [God-ordained] grain of the universe.'"[55] The world is the creation wounded and misdirected toward destructive ends. Accordingly, theologian D. Stephen Long helpfully suggests that we might better, or more precisely and fully, speak of the church-creation / world distinction. Or, in light of apocalyptic, we might even better speak of the church–creation–*new creation* / world distinction.[56]

Notice too that in Paul's and John's accounts, the sin-marred world does not exist simply outside the church. Throughout his letters, and perhaps especially writing to the Corinthians, Paul honestly testifies to sinful worldliness within the churches he counsels. And John is clear: "If we say that we have no sin, we deceive ourselves, and the truth is not in us" (1 John 1:8). In this light, Long is blunt: "*The world is never outside the church.* The world is the capillary flow internal to the church directing our desires from God to false idols, but it is also the condition that allows those desires to be directed to God." Consequently, "the sinfulness of the church also entails that the boundary between church and world cannot be easily fixed."[57]

In creation–new creation as well as in vulnerability to sin, the church then stands in solidarity with the world. There is another aspect of solidarity. Christians, like all other people and like other creatures, still die. The "last enemy" has not yet been destroyed (1 Cor 15:26). So death "remains—however qualified by Christ's

---

55. Long, *Augustinian and Ecclesial*, xxi (emphasis added).

56. Long, 255.

57. Long, 186, 187 (emphasis added).

resurrection—the sign that we live in solidarity with the created order in its finitude and are not yet perfected."[58]

It can hardly be overemphasized that from an apocalyptic perspective, God's work in Christ is first and foremost on behalf of all creation: "Although Paul does not surrender the believer's 'individual' communion with Christ immediately after death, it occupies a secondary position, because Paul's primary concern is the future apocalyptic 'communal' participation of all believers with Christ (1 Thess. 4:17; Rom. 6:8). This points to the solidarity of the whole created order, for just as there is a common solidarity in death, so will there be a common solidarity in eternal life at the time of the final redemption and triumph of God."[59]

Renderings of the Christian story have too often been individualistic and exclusive, not to mention radically anthropocentric. "And so we tend to forget that in the light of God's coming glory and vindication all the creatures of God's world are our neighbors because we share with them not only the suffering of the power of death in this world but also the hope in communal salvation. A responsible apocalyptic recognizes that, without the salvation of our 'neighbor' in the world, our final salvation can be neither asserted nor desired."[60] Outsiders like the atheistic philosopher Alain Badiou may come afresh to Paul's texts and remind us of their central themes. So Badiou, commenting on 1 Corinthians 15:22 (as in Adam all die, in Christ all will be made alive), is not far off when he declares, "There is no place here for vengeance and resentment. Hell, the roasting spit of enemies, holds no interest for Paul." Overall, "justice is copresent in the fidelity of the militant [church], [and]

58. Beker, *Paul the Apostle*, 225.
59. Beker, 230.
60. Beker, *Paul's Apocalyptic Gospel*, 109.

affirms . . . that every victory is in reality a victory for everyone." In sum, "for Paul, it is of utmost importance to declare that I am justified only insofar as everyone is."[61]

As theologian Philip Ziegler puts it, "A Christian theology funded by a fresh hearing of New Testament apocalyptic will acknowledge that it is the world and not the church that is the ultimate object of divine salvation. It will thus conceive of the church as a creation of the Word, a provisional and pilgrim community gathered, upheld, and sent to testify in word and deed to the gospel for the sake of the world. Both individually and corporately, the Christian life is to be understood as militant discipleship in evangelical freedom."[62]

This is an evangelical (i.e., gospel-based and -derived) freedom *from* imprisonment to parochial nationalism and *for* catholicity as well as solidarity with all people—wounded though they be—and with creation as a whole.

---

61. Badiou, *Saint Paul*, 96. Does all this entail universalism? It may, as in David Bentley Hart's emphatic reading; see *That All Shall Be Saved*. But it does not necessarily. To say that God works for the salvation of the whole world and that all persons who are justified are justified in Christ is not necessarily to deny that some people, in their God-granted freedom, may refuse to acknowledge or accept this global and creation-comprehending economy.

62. Ziegler, *Militant Grace*, 29.

6

FREED FROM THE EXPLOITATION OF NATURE, FREED FOR SOLIDARITY WITH CREATION

Both those now commonly designated "liberals" and those designated "conservatives" have roots in a historical, encompassing liberalism. As such, attitudes toward nature—or what I would prefer to call creation—are widely shared across today's partisan political lines. "Liberals" and "conservatives" alike have a heritage of humanity separated from the rest of nature and the reduction of nature to a mere source of "natural resources" to be reaped for human gain.

Karl Polanyi, writing in the mid-twentieth century, warned against the liberal propensity to reduce land to a commodity. Land, he protested, becomes "only another name for nature, which is not produced by man." Such a reduction is in fact "entirely fictitious."[1] But this fiction determined a world picture that set up liberal

1. Polanyi, *Great Transformation*, 75, 76.

humanity to exploit land and nature—now, we see in an age of climate crisis—to our own detriment.

The early liberal attitude to nature is most famously summarized in the words of the Englishman Francis Bacon, a seventeenth-century philosopher, scientist, and statesman. Bacon not only objectified nature but saw nature as an object to be brutally interrogated and raped. So the scientist "must force the apparent facts of nature into forms different to those in which they familiarly present themselves; and thus make them tell the truth about themselves, as torture may compel an unwilling witness to reveal what he has been concealing." Another line, with which feminists have had a field day, advised that "man" should "make no scruple" of "penetrating into [nature's] holes and corners, when the inquisition of truth is his sole object." As Sheldon Wolin encapsulates it, nature for Bacon was "an object of organized assault."[2]

Similarly, clergyman and philosopher William Derham wrote in 1713, "We can, if need be, ransack the whole globe, penetrate into the bowels of the earth, descend to the bottom of the deep, travel to the farthest regions of this world, to acquire wealth." And the Scottish engineer James Watt declared, "Nature can be conquered if we can but find her weak side."[3] The violent subjugation of nature was a strong theme of liberal modernity. As the project proceeded, the forest, to take but one example, morphed from

2. See Deneen, *Why Liberalism Failed*, 72; Klein, *This Changes Everything*, 170; Wolin, *Politics and Vision*, 505. Bacon's view of "man" as the compulsory judge of nature was by no means peculiar to him. Consider Kant: "Reason must approach nature with a view of being instructed by it, though not in the role of a pupil who listens to all that his master chooses to tell him, but in the role of a judge who compels the witnesses to answer questions which he himself thinks fit to pose" (quoted in Taubes, *Occidental Eschatology*, 138).

3. Klein, *This Changes Everything*, 171 and 173.

a multifaceted, wondrous place with its own complex life to an abstraction representing only a saleable volume of lumber or firewood. Scientifically managed "fiscal forests" emerged.

In the German forestry of the late eighteenth and early nineteenth centuries, old forests were felled and cleared. Planted in their place were single species of trees arranged in straight ranks and rows, like an army. As anthropologist and political scientist James C. Scott observes, "The controlled environment of the redesigned, scientific forest promised many striking advantages. It could be synoptically surveyed [from detailed maps] by the chief forester; it could be more easily supervised and harvested according to centralized, long-range plans; it provided a steady, uniform commodity, thereby eliminating one major source of revenue fluctuation; and it created a legible natural terrain that facilitated manipulation and experimentation."[4]

And indeed, many of the pure strands of trees did well in their first generation. But their yields declined sharply in the second generation. The monocropping of trees, the assiduous clearing of underbrush, and the elimination of many apparent "pests" in time upset the intricate, densely webbed and interconnected ecology of the forest. Scott writes, "An exceptionally complex process involving soil building, nutrient uptake, and symbiotic relationships among fungi, insects, mammals, and flora—which were, and still are, not entirely understood—was apparently disrupted, with serious consequences." In short, the forest, conceived solely as a commodity machine, did not work even on its own terms of simply producing a commodity. "The utilitarian commercial and fiscal logic that led to geometric, monocropped, same-age forests . . . led to severe ecological damage. Where the formula had been applied with the greatest

4. Scott, *Seeing like a State*, 18.

149

rigor, it eventually became necessary to attempt to restore much of the forest's original diversity and complexity—or rather, to create a 'virtual' forest that would mimic the robustness and durability of the 'prescientific' forest."[5]

The science of forestry has come a long way since its first generation. And so have many of the other attitudes and practices of humanity in relation to nature. It is now those scornfully dismissed as "liberals" who are the most devout conservationists. But even the most "conservative" would hesitate to speak or act today in the baldly rapacious terms of Bacon, Derham, and Watt. Still, many continue to objectify nature and separate humanity from it. And neoliberals in particular, prone to reinterpret everything in terms of the market, are hard put to see nature as anything other or greater than the provider of "natural resources." Such demeanor inclines one toward the continued exploitation of nature. The "tragic irony" of liberal and neoliberal capitalism is that the very means through which humans sought liberation from the constraints of nature (i.e., fossil-based fuels) is a threat to human and global survival.[6] The effects of air and water pollution, and preeminently the inescapable climate crisis, press upon us all a reconsideration of our heritage. If ecology teaches us that we humans are parts of a rich, variegated, but interconnected web of relationships with the rest of the world—flora and fauna, land and atmosphere—how might we learn to live in solidarity with creation rather than as exploiters of nature?

5. Scott, 20 and 309.
6. See Bretherton, *Christ and the Common Life*, 347.

LETTING CREATION HAVE A VOICE

Theologian and farmer Brian Walsh wants us humans to wake up to the lively expressiveness of the creation that contains, sustains, and suffuses us—of which we are intricately a part. We too easily suppose that rocks and trees, dogs and bees are mute and dumb. They have nothing to say to us. They do not truly interact with us. Utterly objectifying them, we heedlessly lord over them. True enough, we may occasionally employ agential verbs to refer to the nonhuman creation. We say that thunder roars and rocks hit us. But this is figurative, "merely poetic" language. In fact, creation possesses no voice or volition.

Walsh, however, subverts the relegation of all such language to the "merely poetic" (as if there were such a thing) by turning to the eminently modern practice and substance of science. Writing alongside a trained forester, Walsh shows that trees are "responsive creatures." Cooperating with neighboring fungi, trees actively enhance their own and the fungi's existence. Fungus assists trees by absorbing nitrogen and phosphorous and, in return, receives the trees' surplus carbohydrates. Furthermore, trees communicate with one another through the vast underground "train systems" of the fungi. For instance, a tree may warn nearby trees that an endangering pest has invaded it and may soon invade them. It is time to ramp up chemical systems that may repel or eliminate the pest.

No less fascinatingly, Walsh and his coauthors write, "Trees display qualities totally inexplicable if considered solely from a mechanistic, nonresponsive viewpoint. For example, a mechanical model could lead us to reasonably expect that tree growth could be predicted accurately and that foresters could create an 'ideotype' or model tree. The fact that foresters cannot do this and that trees of the same species growing in the same soil, climate, and spacing conditions seem to respond individually to the same stimuli suggests that there is something else in trees—a selfhood, or subjectivity, or a factor 'x'—contributing to their infinite variety."[7]

Walsh attributes individuality, "selfhood," and "subjectivity" to trees. In the same spirit, he and his coauthors cite the Nobel Prize–winning work of botanical geneticist Barbara McClintock. She scrutinized the corn plant as "a unique individual," "a mysterious other," and "a kindred subject." "This 'kindred subjectivity' is a 'special kind of attention that most of us experience only in relation to other persons'; as J. B. McDaniel explains, corn plants to McClintock 'are distant, perhaps very distant cousins: strange but lovable kin.'"[8]

Of course, Walsh is a theologian. His ultimate aim is to argue that Christians especially should recover a sense of the nonhuman creation as truly alive, responsive, and subjective. The biblical witness entails nothing less. In a particularly sweeping and pregnant passage, Walsh, with coauthor Sylvia Keesmaat, proclaims,

> In stark contrast to the anthropocentric preoccupations of both modernity and postmodernity, biblical faith affirms that creation is an eloquent gift of extravagant love. This is not a world of objects that sit mutely waiting for the human subject to master them. Rather, this is a world of created fellow subjects, all called into being by the same Creator, all born of the Creator's love, all included in the Creator's covenant of creational restoration, and all responsive agents in the kingdom

7. Walsh, Karsh, and Ansell, "Trees, Forestry." For an engrossing novelistic exploration of trees' subjectivity and agency, see Powers, *Overstory*.

8. Walsh, Karsh, and Ansell, "Trees, Forestry."

of the beloved Son. . . . A creation called into being by the Word of God, created in, through and for Christ in whom all creation coheres, is not a mechanistic system but a dynamic, personal, living creation that has a voice.[9]

This is exactly and thoroughly right. In what follows, I unpack Keesmaat and Walsh's assertions. Nonhuman creation, theologically considered, is "eloquent." It is "a world of created fellow subjects." All creatures are "responsive agents." Creation is "dynamic, personal, living," and it "has a voice." Indeed, and though Keesmaat and Walsh do not use this language, I will press further and argue that we should embrace nothing less than a Christian animism—seeing the more-than-human creation not as mechanistic or inert but as genuinely alive—that is, *animate*.

REDEMPTION AND ECOLOGY

The Bible has not always been read in an ecologically sensitive manner. But I hope to show that it can be.[10] Obviously, the biblical witness provides grounds for a doctrine of creation that includes nonhuman creation, from Genesis 1 onward. So we will instead begin with the themes of soteriology and eschatology. It has been assumed that salvation is simply and solely for human beings. But this assumption is obtuse and shortchanges the biblical testimony.[11]

9. Keesmaat and Walsh, *Colossians Remixed*, 123.

10. For an excellent introduction to an ecologically attuned reading of the Bible, see Horrell, *Bible and the Environment*.

11. For a more detailed consideration of the following, see my *New Creation*. Consider also the seminal works of Middleton, *New Heaven*; and Wright, *Surprised by Hope*.

Remember our apocalyptic framing. In Jesus's life, death, and resurrection, the kingdom of God has come. Through the cross, the saints have "been set free from the present evil age" (Gal 1:4). Because the Messiah has died and risen from the dead, "the ends of the ages has come" (1 Cor 10:11). Everything old has passed away, and there is a new creation (2 Cor 5:17).

With Jesus, the kingdom has been inaugurated, but it has not yet been manifested in its fullness. We look ahead to Jesus's parousia, when God will raise the dead into transformed, new bodies (1 Cor 15). More than this, we look ahead to a new heaven and a new earth. The apostle Peter anticipates Jesus's return, which will effectuate the *"universal restoration* that God announced long ago through his holy prophets" (Acts 3:21). Second Peter 3:13 similarly declares that "in accordance with [God's] promise, we wait for new heavens and a new earth, where righteousness is at home." Revelation likewise expects "a new heaven and a new earth" (Rev 21:1) and the New Jerusalem, the city of God that descends to earth, to include a rolling river that nourishes trees of life (Rev 22:2). At the fullness of time, the Letter to the Ephesians says, God "will gather up all things in [Christ], things in heaven and things on earth" (Eph 1:10).

At more length, the apostle Paul apocalyptically writes,

For the creation waits with eager longing for the revealing of the children of God; for the creation was subjected to futility, not of its own will but by the will of the one who subjected it, in hope that the creation itself will be set free from its bondage to decay and will obtain the freedom of the glory of the children of God. We know that the whole creation has been groaning in labor pains until now; and not only the creation, but we ourselves, who have the first fruits of the Spirit, groan inwardly while we wait for adoption, the redemption of our bodies. (Rom 8:19–23)[12]

In their hope for a new heaven and a new earth, the New Testament writers draw on a rich trove of Old Testament traditions. Isaiah 11 foresees the famous peaceable kingdom, with animals living in harmony with one another and humans. Jeremiah 31:27 declares, "The days are surely coming, says the Lord, when I will sow the house of Israel and the house of Judah with the seed of humans *and the seed of animals*." Hosea 2:18 understands God's covenant to encompass the more-than-human animals: "I will make for you a covenant on that day with the wild animals, the birds of the air, and the creeping things of the ground; and I will abolish the bow, the sword, and war from the land; and I will make you lie down in safety." Accordingly, Psalm 36:5–6 exults,

> Your steadfast love, O Lord, extends to the heavens,
>   your faithfulness to the clouds.
> Your righteousness is like the mighty mountains,
>   your judgments are like the great deep;
>   you save humans *and animals* [emphasis added] alike.

We need not look far for the origins of this biblical sensitivity to the whole of creation. The ancient Israelites were a people of the land. And their land was steep, rocky, and semiarid. Droughts came to pass every three years out of ten. There was little room for

---

12. Theologian Sarah Coakley comments on this text: "What this underscores is the extraordinary ripple effect of prayer in the Spirit—its inexorably social and even cosmic significance as an act of cooperation with, and incorporation into, the still extending life of the incarnation" (*God, Sexuality*, 114).

error—and no margin for oblivious waste—in their gardening and farming. They knew they depended on the earth and its bounty for their welfare; if it suffered, so did they. Thus the Israelites were necessarily, and exquisitely, ecologically sensitive.

For the health of the soil, they let the land lie fallow at regular intervals (Exod 23:11). They took care of their own livestock (Deut 25:4) and that of their neighbors (Deut 22:4). And they were solicitous of wildlife, which sometimes also provided sustenance: "If you come on a bird's nest, in any tree or on the ground, with fledglings or eggs, with the mother sitting on the fledglings or on the eggs, you shall not take the mother with the young. Let the mother go, taking only the young for yourself, in order that it may go well with you and you may live long" (Deut 22:6–7).

But the Israelites were also capable of considering the nonhuman creation's welfare in distinction from their own. Their creation story imagined that God created flora and fauna and declared it good *before* the existence of humanity (Gen 1). They saw God's beneficent creation and provision extending to "every wild animal," "creeping things," wild goats, coneys, and lions (Ps 104)—aspects of creation that were quite apart from providing any human resource or use. In addition, as I will elaborate, creation by its very being is understood to offer praise to God. In other words, God would not lack praise and honor even if creation included no human beings. In the biblical vision, nonhuman creation is neither mute nor ungrateful.[13]

Jesus inherits the ecological heritage of Israel. He manifestly had an intuitively ecological, agrarian sensibility of humanity's place within a larger, undergirding, and surrounding creation. His

---

13. Nor necessarily sinful or fallen, though clearly "subjected," as Paul writes in Rom 8:20. See Garvey, *God's Good Earth*.

teachings drip with creaturely resonances. His parables draw often from the farmer's world: seeds and growth in different qualities of soil, planting and harvest, wheat infested with weeds. He allays human anxiety with an appeal to the demeanor and behavior of other creatures, alluding to the cheapest of birds, the sparrows, not one of whom is "forgotten in God's sight" (Luke 12:6–7). Likewise, he is sensitive to the lilies of the field, which "neither toil nor spin" but are clothed in stupendous beauty (Matt 6:25–30).

Nor should we neglect, in these regards, a key event in Jesus's life, the temptation in the wilderness. For the biblical cultures, the wilderness (among its more benign properties) was dangerous to humans and seen as the haunt of demons (Isa 13:21–22, 34:1–5; Rev 18:2). This is crucial background to Mark's brief account of the temptation, which, in our translation (NRSV), comprises a single sentence: "He was in the wilderness forty days, tempted by Satan; *and he was with the wild beasts*; and the angels waited on him" (1:13; emphasis added).[14] At Jesus's baptism, he is anointed with the Spirit and identified as God's Son, thus embedding him in the lineage of King David not only genealogically (Matt 1:1) but spiritually and politically (see Ps 2:7–8). Now he goes to confront Satan directly on his own territory.

Mark's account is terse but extremely suggestive. It breaks Jesus's sojourn in the wilderness into three encounters. First, he was with Satan. Second, "he was with the wild beasts." Third, "the angels waited on him." Satan is Jesus's implacable foe. The angels are his friends. In between, he is with the wild beasts. Jesus does not tame or domesticate them; he is merely "with" them. Such beasts, in the Palestinian desert of Jesus's time, would have included bears,

14. For the following exegesis, I am indebted to Bauckham, *Living with Other Creatures*, 111–32.

leopards, wolves, cobras, desert vipers, scorpions, hyenas, jackals, desert lynx, foxes, wild boars, wild asses, antelopes, gazelles, wild goats, porcupines, and rabbits. In the Greek translated "he was with," we have the sense of a close, benign presence. Jesus does not leash the leopard or cuddle the jackal. But in a way, he befriends them, letting them be what they are.

Jesus confronts Satan and makes peace with the wild animals (with resonances of Isaiah 11) before he proclaims and enacts the kingdom of God among humans. It is as if he establishes his messianic and apocalyptic bona fides with nonhuman creation, only then entering the human arena as the Anointed One. His peaceful sojourn among the wild animals may be likened to his later healing ministry. He does not, with a mass gesture, heal every sick person in Israel. Inaugurating the kingdom of God, he heals some and so signals the later healing of all in the eschaton. Likewise, Jesus's presence among the wild beasts for forty days does not once and for all make the wilderness safe for any and all subsequent wanderers. But it too is a sign of the inauguration of the kingdom awaiting its fullness. How marvelous that it includes the animal kingdom as well as the human and demonic kingdoms.

Finally, in this dash through the biblical ecological story, we should not forget that God on occasion embodies or acts through nonhuman creation. God engages Moses in the form of a burning bush (Exod 3:4–6). Supremely, the Holy Spirit descends on the baptized Jesus "in bodily form like a dove" (Luke 3:21–22). In the Old Testament, the dove is a symbol of God's compassion, a "divine emissary and guardian of sacred order," a "living embodiment of God's protection, healing, and love" (Gen 8:6–12, 15; Song 2:14, 4:1, 5:2, 6:9; Ezek 7:16; Jer 48:28).[15] As the ecotheologian

---

15. Wallace, *When God Was a Bird*, 27.

Mark Wallace astutely notes, "Gently alighting on Jesus's person, just like the creation bird hovering over the deep in Genesis, the Gospels' heaven-sent dovey pigeon is God enfleshing Godself in carnal form, but now not only in human flesh in the person of Jesus (God's Son) but also in animal flesh in the person of the Spirit (God's Spirit)."[16]

All told, nonhuman creation is very much included in the biblical story. Considered doctrinally, this is true in terms of creation (all is created good), of soteriology and eschatology (all of creation is liberated in Christ), of the incarnation (of the Son and, in a different manner—Christ assumes and becomes a body once and for all, while the Spirit becomes dove only temporarily—the Spirit), and of pneumatology (the Spirit as pigeon). The vision induced and conveyed by the biblical story is profoundly ecological. Humans exist in an animate, dynamic matrix of which they are never independent. All of creation is suffused and enlivened by *ruach*, the breath or wind or atmosphere of God. Humans breathe and ingest nonhuman creation; they are part of it, and it is part of them. In the Christian story, as noted in an earlier chapter, creation is triply sanctified. First, creation is made good and delightful. Second, Jesus's incarnation blesses all creation and not just humans. Third, his victorious resurrection liberates all of creation. As the Eastern Orthodox theologian Paulos Mar Gregorios succinctly puts it, "Christ the Incarnate One assumed flesh—organic, human flesh; he was nurtured by air and water, vegetables and meat, like the rest of us. He took matter into himself, so matter is not alien to him now. His body is a *material* body—transformed, of course, but transformed *matter*. Thus he shares his being with the whole created order: animals and birds, snakes and worms, flowers and seeds. All parts of creation are

16. Wallace, 31.

now reconciled to Christ. And the created order is set free to share in the glorious freedom of the children of God."[17]

A CHRISTIAN ANIMISM

We are now well poised to say what may properly be meant by a Christian animism. First, as Wallace is careful to say, Christian animism is

> not pantheism—nor is it unadulterated animism per se. On the contrary, the model of animism in a biblical register . . . alternately sounds two different but complementary notes: the enfleshment of God in the world vis-à-vis Jesus's humanity and the Spirit's animality, on the one hand, and the alterity of God in God's self as heterogeneous to the world, on the other. Christian animism does not elide the differences between God and the world—as can happen in some pantheistic and animistic formulations of the God-world relationship—insofar as God and world are not collapsed into the same reality without remainder. Instead, it sets forth both the continuity and discontinuity between the divine life and earthly existence.[18]

Christian animism is open and sensitive to God's immanence but does not neglect or in any way deny God's transcendence. God and creation are not identical or coterminous.[19] God is indeed wholly

---

17. Cited in Linzey and Regan, *Animals and Christianity*, 27.

18. Wallace, *When God Was a Bird*, 15.

19. Though Wallace at places clearly affirms the radical difference between God and creation, he can at times seem to perilously elide this difference. So at one

other than God's creation. The Trinitarian God is not lonely, lacking, or in need. Instead, creation is an act of God's graciousness and abundant, overflowing love.

For Christian animism too there can be no true or robust understanding of how nonhuman creation is alive and sentient apart from God's dealings with Israel and in Christ's apocalypse. In other words, a very human and linguistic mediation is necessary and prior. It is the biblical story that enables us to construe the God-world relation lucidly and rightly. And the Bible is the church's book. So a Christian animism has no place for replacing or substituting (human) ecclesiological involvement with nature as the "church."[20]

With these essential qualifiers in hand, we may affirm the sense in which the biblical cultures were animistic. We must not forget that these cultures were predominantly oral and indigenous—that is, most people did not read and write or depart far from their places of origin. They were grounded in and intimately connected to nonhuman creation. And as the phenomenologist David Abram notes, for indigenous oral cultures, "nature itself is articulate; it *speaks*. The human voice in an oral culture is always to some extent participant with the voices of wolves, wind, and wave—participant, that

---

point he suggests that if humanity somehow destroys the earth, God may be killed in the process (162–69). I demur here.

20. Here again I may be departing from Wallace. His chapter on John Muir is rich and edifying but troubling. He is illuminating on how the young Muir was immersed in Scripture and argues forcefully that Muir's animism was informed, even formed, by ecclesial mediation. But he seems to imply that it was fine for the adult Muir to leave behind the (human) church and replace it with the church as nature. Wallace can even write, with emphasis and apparently approvingly, "*For Muir, then, nature is baptism. Nature is church. Nature is redemption. Nature is God*" (125). I strongly disavow all four of these affirmations.

is, with the encompassing discourse of an animate earth. There is no element of the landscape that is definitively void of expressive resonance and power: any movement may be a gesture, any sound may be a voice, a meaningful utterance."[21]

As Abram elsewhere puts it, "While persons brought up within literate culture often speak *about* the natural world, indigenous, oral peoples sometimes speak directly *to* that world, acknowledging certain animals, plants, and even landforms as expressive subjects with whom they might find themselves in conversation."[22] As we will see shortly, the expressiveness of nature and the possibility of directly addressing and conversing with it are represented in the biblical text. Abram stresses that the animism of oral peoples was participatory. Rather than seeing themselves as entirely separate from and independent of nature, the ancient Israelites and Jews of Jesus's day vividly encountered and engaged the natural world and felt themselves encountered and engaged by the natural world. As Abram says, "Careful attention to the evidence suggests that ancient Hebraic religiosity was far more corporeal, and far more responsive to the sensuous earth, than we commonly assume."[23]

But ours is a predominately literate, not oral, culture. Does this mean we must be out of reach of a Christian animist sensibility? Immersed in alphabetic writing, we do have, in comparison to oral peoples, an extra layer between our experience of the world—and of nonhuman creation in particular. We are insulated in a way the oral peoples were not. Yet Abram argues that we are not entirely shut up, or hermetically sealed, in written language. We still encounter weather, nurture plants, touch and are

21. Abram, *Spell of the Sensuous*, 116–17.
22. Abram, *Becoming Animal*, 10.
23. Abram, *Spell of the Sensuous*, 240.

touched by animals. Much of our science, such as that of Barbara McClintock's, demonstrates that we can still learn from and listen to nonhuman creation in a kind of conversation. We can still be inspired, challenged, transformed, and renewed by our engagements with creation in its many forms. Thus Abram seems right in suggesting that the human organism has "a spontaneous propensity" for sensitive participation with the nonhuman world. This is a participation that is "radically transformed, *yet not eradicated*, by alphabetic writing."[24] Consider the following meditation by the twentieth-century monk Thomas Merton: "The rain surrounded the cabin . . . with a whole world of meaning, of secrecy, of rumor. Think of it: all that speech pouring down, selling nothing, judging nobody, drenching the thick mulch of dead leaves, soaking the trees, filling the gullies and crannies of the wood with water, washing out places where men have stripped the hillsides. . . . Nobody started it, nobody is going to stop it. It will talk as long as it wants, the rain. As long as it talks I am going to listen."[25]

Immersed and insulated in literacy and enamored of a highly technological world that literally screens us off from the rest of creation, we can easily forget that we are finely participant in and with nature. Our reconnection to the nonhuman world will not come without intention and effort.[26] But as Merton shows, we need not necessarily remain oblivious—and with the climate crisis, the natural world is more and more intensely and insistently demanding our attention. With that said, let us listen afresh to the biblical text.

24. Abram, 176 (emphasis added).
25. Quoted in Abram, 73.
26. For some counsel to that end, see Abram, *Becoming Animal*, 288–92.

ANIMISTIC BIBLICAL TEXTS

In Genesis, in the primeval murder, Cain kills his brother Abel. The ground on which the crime occurs responds actively. It swallows Abel's blood and issues a curse, refusing thereafter to "yield . . . its strength" when Cain tills it (Gen 4:11–12). Similarly, in Leviticus, the people are warned against committing abominations, lest "the land . . . vomit you out for defiling it" (Lev 18:28). In other texts too, because of human sin, the earth mourns, dries up, withers (Jer 4:28, 14:1–6; Hos 4:3). It is not much of a stretch to read such texts and imagine the earth's response to global warming. The human defilement of creation results in the atmosphere's rejoinder of vomiting out (or burning out) its human inhabitants. Creation's suffering at human obduracy and obscurity must have been something of what the apostle Paul had in mind when he wrote of creation "groaning" for its release from futility (Rom 8:10–23).

We have already noted Hosea 2:18, where God promises a covenant with nonhuman creation. Here we may add Joshua 24:27, where Joshua sets up a stone as "a witness against us; for it has heard all the words of the Lord that he spoke to us; therefore it shall be a witness against you, if you deal falsely with your God." In the biblical animistic vision, creation is addressable and responsible. In this vein, the prophet Ezekiel is commanded to "prophesy to the mountains of Israel. . . . Therefore, O mountains of Israel, hear the word of the Lord God" (Ezek 36:1, 4). And nonhuman creation—by contrast with human creation—is portrayed as always faithful to its calling to covenant, witness, and prophecy: "Faithfulness will spring up from the ground, and righteousness will look down from the sky. The Lord will give what is good, and our land will yield its increase" (Ps 85:11–12). In this mentality, Jesus responds to the

Pharisees, who want the acclamatory crowd to shut up: "I tell you, if these were silent, the stones would shout out" (Luke 19:34–40).

In like manner, Job commissions conversation with creation:

> But ask the animals, and they will teach you;
>> the birds of the air, and they will tell you;
> ask the plants of the earth, and they will teach you;
>> and the fish of the sea will declare to you. (Job 12:7–8)

Out of its inherent wisdom and faithfulness, the addressable creation is ready to praise God and exultant with praise:

> Let the sea roar, and all that fills it;
>> the world and those who live in it.
> Let the floods clap their hands;
>> let the hills sing together for joy
> at the presence of the Lord, for he is coming
>> to judge the earth.
> He will judge the world with righteousness,
>> and the peoples with equity. (Ps 98:7–9)

> Praise the Lord from the earth,
>> you sea monsters and all deeps,
> fire and hail, snow and frost,
>> stormy wind fulfilling his command!

> Mountains and all hills,
>> fruit trees and all cedars!
> Wild animals and all cattle,
>> creeping things and flying birds! (Ps 148:7–10)

For you shall go out in joy
  and be led back in peace;
the mountains and the hills before you
  shall burst into song,
  and all the trees of the field shall clap their hands. (Isa 55:12)

Like all orally oriented people, the biblical cultures are vigorously participant in the creation that embeds and surrounds them. They experience creation as conversant and responsive, addressable by God and by themselves. Their catalog of responsive creation bursts in comprehensiveness, including all manner of created entities: the ground, the skies, stones, trees, clouds, mountains and hills, plants and trees, creeping things, domesticated and wild animals, birds, seas and floods, water-dwelling creatures, fire, hail, snow, frost, wind, and atmospheric storms. Creation is agential and can only be described with an abundance of verbs. It variously witnesses, groans, tells, teaches, declares, yields, praises, hears, waits, swallows, vomits, curses, mourns, sings, claps, roars, and looks. Accordingly, it is a participant in the covenant.

And let us note again, it is constant in its faithfulness and ever eager to praise. Simply by being themselves, all creatures exult in the abundant life given to them by God. As Karl Barth puts it, non-human creatures praise God "along with us or without us. They do it also against us to shame us and instruct us." By comparison, the human "is only like a late-comer slipping shamefacedly into creation's choir in heaven and earth, which has never ceased its praise, but merely suffered and sighed, as it still does, that in inconceivable folly and ingratitude its living centre man does not hear its voice, its response, its echoing of the divine glory, or rather hears it in a completely perverted way, and refuses to co-operate in the jubilation which surrounds him."[27] The nineteenth-century Catholic poet Gerard Manley Hopkins wonderfully captured this sense of an animate, worshipping creation in a single stanza:

> As kingfishers catch fire, dragonflies draw flame;
> As tumbled over rim in roundy wells
> Stones ring; like each tucked string tells, each hung bell's
> Bow swung finds tongue to fling out broad its name;
> Each mortal thing does one thing and the same:
> Deals out that being indoors each one dwells;
> Selves—goes itself; *myself* it speaks and spells,
> Crying *Whát I dó is me: for that I came.*[28]

RELEARNING HOW TO HEAR CREATION'S VOICE

Human solidarity with all of creation is twofold. First, humans are created by God with all other creatures. Second, humans, like the entirety of creation, are created toward the end of worshipping and praising God. We are creatures alongside other creatures. And those creatures, like us, find their fulfillment in the worship of the God of Israel and Jesus Christ. When we exploit creation, we abuse fellow creatures and coworshippers.

An apocalyptic frame disallows seeing the earth as a wreck from which some human individuals are rescued. Instead, Christ's apocalyptic work is about the re-creation of the cosmos, human and nonhuman, toward the end that it be in proper relationship with

27. Barth, *Church Dogmatics* II/1, 648.
28. Hopkins, "Inversnaid," 51.

God and its myriad cocreatures and coworshippers. Nor do we correctly understand apocalypse if we imagine creation—except for some lucky humans—being destroyed, consumed in fire. The apocalyptic fire is a purifying and transforming fire, not one of simple destruction. As J. Christiaan Beker puts it, "The apostle [Paul] is not charged with simply pronouncing the end of the world to the world. Rather that charge must be executed in the context of enlarging in this world the domain of God's coming world because God's coming world envisages *the transformation* of the world's present structures and not simply their dissolution."[29]

Stephen Long helpfully expands, "All of creation is in some sense graced; it is intrinsic to its nature as God's gift. The church is the site in which that nature can be seen for what it is because of what it should be. It is the repetitive apocalyptic inbreaking found in Word and Sacrament by which God visits God's people and makes them God's own. This 'inbreaking' does not destroy nature, only its fallen accidents, but restores and perfects it." In short, apocalyptic "eschatology is the vindication of creation, not its destruction."[30]

Accordingly, in the face of neoliberal capitalism, which envisions creation only as exploitable nature, an apocalyptic perspective calls the church and the world to exercise not merely or primarily power over creation but power with creation. We may—we must—long and work for an economics that responds to creation gently and attentively. And as the climate crisis demonstrates, we must work for a sustainable economics, not one that assumes and promotes infinite growth in a finite world. Such an economics "does not idolize or fetishize nature, but it affirms that salvation is cosmic in scope, and it enacts a participation in Christ in which the sacramentality

29. Beker, *Paul's Apocalyptic Gospel*, 57.
30. Long, *Augustinian and Ecclesial*, 155 and 249–50.

of all nature is affirmed in proclaiming God's glory. The question is not so much whether we are to evangelize nature as whether we will allow ourselves to evangelize *with* nature and to be evangelized *by* nature"—which already, by biblical testimony, is constantly and copiously praising God.[31]

All told, though we need not deny the place of the market, we must recognize that it does have a place—not as the all-encompassing and all-defining framework of being but as within, limited, and constrained by a surrounding and suffusing social and ecological matrix. Within that matrix, it should serve the rightful and prospering ends of society and all of creation. Its own survival depends on this. James Scott expresses it well:

> The market is itself an instituted, formal system of coordination, despite the elbow room that it provides its participants, and it is therefore . . . dependent on a larger system of social relations which its own calculus does not acknowledge and which it can neither create nor maintain. Here I have in mind not only the obvious elements of contract and property law, as well as the state's coercive power to enforce them, but antecedent patterns and norms of social trust, community, and cooperation, without which market exchange is inconceivable. *Finally, and most important, the economy is "a sub-system of a finite and nongrowing eco-system," whose carrying capacity and interactions it must respect as a condition of its own persistence.*[32]

At the behest of an unrestrained market, we have in just over two centuries depleted goods it took millions of years for nature

---

31. Stone, *Evangelism after Christendom*, 220.
32. Scott, *Seeing like a State*, 351 (internal quote from Herman Daly; emphasis added).

to accrue. Future generations may look back on us and, mashing up the verb *squander* and the noun *scoundrel*, call us something like "squandrels." In any event, the damage already done by climate change is considerable. Beyond the overwhelming science, we can see with our own eyes the melting ice caps or the ice fishers unable to venture onto Lake Michigan in the winters of 2019 and 2020. Creation is speaking, even shouting now. How much more blessed we will be—cocreatures and coworshippers all, men and women, rocks and trees, dogs and bees—if humans relearn how to hear creation's voice, not just at a scream, but at a whisper.

7

FREED FROM THE FEAR OF DEATH, FREED FOR LIFE AS GIFT

Neoliberals preach that in terms of ordering our lives and understanding ourselves, the market is the best framework humans can achieve. Yet the neoliberal social imaginary cannot encompass a central fact of human destiny: all humans die. In response, neoliberals on the ground can only deny aging and rage against its endpoint of death. For example, as the social critic Barbara Ehrenreich observes, "Silicon Valley's towering hubris demands nothing less than immortality."[1] So every day, the wealthy futurist Ray Kurzweil swallows 250 pills containing nutritional supplements and every week goes to a clinic where supplements are intravenously delivered into his bloodstream. By these means, he hopes to prolong his life until about 2040, when he expects biomedical breakthroughs in the form of disease-fighting nanobots that will be injected into our bloodstreams and prolong life indefinitely.[2]

1. Ehrenreich, *Natural Causes*, 79.
2. Ehrenreich, 79.

Similarly, the billionaire Peter Thiel, cofounder of PayPal, plans to live to the age of 120. Dmitry Itskov, the "godfather" of the Russian internet, has a goal of living to 10,000. Sergey Brin, cofounder of Oracle, hopes someday to "cure death." And Larry Ellison, cofounder of Oracle, finds accepting mortality "incomprehensible." Ellison expresses his gargantuan sense of entitlement explicitly, saying, "Death makes me very angry," and has spent hundreds of millions to fund antiaging research.[3]

But so long as death remains inevitable, the neoliberal economy can only resist and delay it. Death cannot be embraced or overcome in this "religion." It can only provoke fear and fear's close cousin, anger. The Christian perspective is different. Its horizon exceeds the neoliberal horizon and reaches beyond death while in no way denying its reality. As the theologian Kathryn Tanner puts it, "In maximum contrast to the short-term time horizons of profiteering in [neoliberal] finance-dominated capitalism, here one's time horizon is exceedingly long. In acting now one imagines oneself, for example, brought before God's judgment seat after death." And one participates in the communion of saints, past and dead as well as present and alive.[4]

APOCALYPTIC AND DEATH'S THROW WEIGHT

A Christian apocalyptic intervention plays out in a wider economy—God's economy—where death has been confronted and defeated. The New Testament scholar Martinus De Boer finds three aspects or meanings of death in Jewish apocalyptic literature, aspects the apostle Paul adopts in his own eschatological

3. Ehrenreich, 80.
4. Tanner, *Christianity and the New Spirit*, 128.

understanding.[5] This is but to say that death's throw weight is trifold and considerable.

The first aspect of death is the literal, physical demise of the body in and through which we live and breathe and praise God. The second aspect Boer calls moral death, where sin and unrighteous behavior separate even the physically living from God. One may be the walking dead in sin (Rom 8:10). The third aspect is eschatological death, or eternal separation from God—in a word, perdition. All three deaths threaten separation from God, the source of life. Theologically, nothing worse can be imagined. "Physical, moral, and eschatological death are different facets of death's all-embracing hegemony." And none is remediable through human effort.[6]

Old and new "apocalyptic" perspectives create timetables for the end times, range heroic angels against villainous demons, and rejoice in the eschatological suffering of defeated oppressors. But as Beker notes, Paul "does not engage in apocalyptic timetables, descriptions of the architecture of heaven, or accounts of demons and angels; nor does he take delight in the rewards of the blessed and the torture of the wicked (cf. Revelation). The major apocalyptic forces are, for him, those ontological powers that determine the human situation within the context of God's created order and that comprise the 'field' of death, sin, the law, and the flesh."[7]

The greatest or primal power within these interlocking forces is death, what Paul calls the "last enemy" (1 Cor 15:26). In his own death, Christ has confronted and undergone the power of the last enemy, and he has risen to vanquish it. This confrontation has not merely a moral but an ontological result. At the very basic level

---

5. De Boer, *Defeat of Death*, 83–84, 181–84.

6. De Boer, 184.

7. Beker, *Paul the Apostle*, 189.

of being, everything has changed through Christ's dying and rising again. Sin and death, these underlying powers threatening always to separate us from God and life, have been defeated. "For Paul, the death and resurrection of Christ are cosmic-ontological events. The resurrection has inaugurated a new ontological reality, that is, the reality of resurrection life as the new creation that—however proleptic—has changed the nature of historical reality."[8] Accordingly, even now, "Christian flesh has decisively moved from death to life. The deaths it still inflicts [as in the consumption of animals] and the death it will itself undergo are remnants, threads in a slaughter-fabric being unpicked by Jesus and rewoven into a garment of light and life."[9]

Death—physical, moral, and eschatological—has been overthrown and can no longer, in any of its forms, "separate us from the love of God in Christ Jesus our Lord" (Rom 8:39). At the same time, apocalyptic, while full-throatedly proclaiming the defeat of death, does not in any way deny its lingering effects or "remnants." Still, wars rage, fathers abuse children, lethal violence ensues, cancers run rampant, people perish from hunger, and so on, and so on. "The empirical evidence for this 'not yet' is everywhere evident and irrefutable. The believer, however, knows that in Christ God *has* already defeated these powers and, for that very reason, *will* do so—not simply at some distant or not so distant future point in time, though that too, but whenever and wherever faith occurs."[10]

The Christian with Paul's apocalyptic perspective then looks at all reality "bifocally."[11] On the one hand, she looks unsentimentally

---

8. Beker, 196.

9. Griffiths, *Christian Flesh*, 104.

10. De Boer, *Defeat of Death*, 178.

11. See Martyn, *Galatians*, 104.

at the world and sees its darkness and sometimes diabolical brokenness. She refuses to turn away from the ravages of pain and death and is always prepared for service in their face. On the other hand, she knows that Christ is and will be the victor, and she gathers the courage to confront injustice, oppression, and sin in all its manifestations over and over again. She is at once vulnerable to suffering and open to joy. Her hope is not mere optimism but a hard-won confidence that ultimately, amid all the setbacks, the long arc of God's universe bends toward justice, peace, and wholeness. To put it otherwise, she knows the reality at its bottom is now cross-shaped and that at the cross, death does its worst but does not have the last word.

So it is that the economy of God, centered on Christ, encompasses and subsumes death.

DEATH AND LIBERATION FROM SLAVERY

The fear of death, in the sense of physical demise, is innate or instinctual to the human organism. Even Freud, who speculated that we have death drives, saw in the human psyche a profound tendency toward life and self-preservation. Psychologists and biologists speak of an instinctual "fight or flight" response to danger, a basic propensity, one way or another, to end the imminent threat. How can we not feel fear, experience peak anxiety, in the face of death? Who has not flown in heavy weather—the plane dropping and lifting like a manic elevator, the lightning bolts outside the window wide and bone white—and failed to grip the armrest, say a prayer, perhaps utter a cry? My primal death fear, the most urgent and despairing in my imagination, is that of being attacked by a shark. It has something to do with the animal's blank and unexpressive eyes, with so much of its body devoted to piercing teeth and wide jaws—all the better to bite and swallow whole. And it has something to do with the shark's origins from the murky and unknown depths, into which it would drag me down. So it is that we imagine death, or come close to it, and feel a faster-beating heart, hyperalertness, accelerated breathing, sweat on the palms of our hands.

Above all else, death is a confrontation with the unknown, or at least the radically unfamiliar. It takes courage to learn how to ride a bicycle, as the early, wobbling attempts are met with the distinct possibility of injury. But in time, the child masters balance, and fear is overtaken by delight at gliding along. Death is different. It comes once, without any actual rehearsal.[12]

Theologically, however, this is not entirely true. Baptism is a kind of death and a passage from death into new life. So Christians in their baptisms rehearse dying in a real fashion. Yet this is largely ignored in our typical modern baptisms, especially infant baptisms, which usually verge on the sentimental and the cute. When water is poured over the babe's head, contemporary Christians often ooh and ah. Clearly, they are not imagining the child's death by drowning. Still, at least in my tradition (Episcopal), the actual baptismal vows and prayers do not ignore death and its power.

The baptismal covenant is a responsive recitation of the Apostles' Creed, which affirms that Christ died on the cross and was buried, dead as dead can be—and then he rose. The Prayers for the Candidates begin with "Deliver them, O Lord, from the way of

---

12. The outliers here are those who have near-death experiences. If they in fact experience what should rightly be called death, and that is debated, they do have a sort of rehearsal. And at least those with benign experiences report a new calmness, even serenity, in the face of their eventual demise. For a masterful treatment, see Zaleski, *Otherworld Journeys*.

sin and death." The Thanksgiving over the Water recognizes that in the water of baptism, "we are buried with Christ in his death."[13]

Former generations of Christians were often franker and more fulsome in their recognition of death. Cleaning their combs, they might grasp the loose hairs and associate them with their eventual physical demise. In their baptisms and imagination, they rehearsed their future deaths.

But did they thereby altogether eliminate the fear of death? I doubt it. What they may have learned was an increased courage in the face of death. Note that courage is not the absence of fear but its mastery. Failing to experience fear where fear is appropriate is not the virtue of courage; it is the vice of foolhardiness. What matters, or what we might most fittingly aim for, is not the total absence of feelings of fear in the face of death but again a sort of bifocal vision, on the one hand seeing death in all its fearsome power, and on the other hand also seeing it overcome in Christ's cross and resurrection. We might not erase all fearful emotions, yet we might master the fears and proceed in the face of death. We might no longer be frozen or take flight in death's shadow.

Ineluctably, even with faith, what we *know* about death and its beyond is not much. Yet a pioneer has gone before us into this cloudy unknown and has emerged to lead us through it (Heb 2:10; 12:2). The path, though still fearsome, has been broken and trodden on our behalf: "Since, therefore, the children share flesh and blood, he himself likewise shared the same things, so that through death he might destroy the one who has the power of death, that is, the devil, and free those who all their lives were held in slavery by the fear of death" (Heb 2:14–15). What Christ eliminates for us, most precisely put, is not the fear of death—in the face of which

---

13. Episcopal Church, *Book of Common Prayer*, 304–6.

he himself underwent anxiety and agony—but slavery to the fear of death. We are liberated from this slavery, and so are no longer determined in our being or actions by the power of death. And that has been the case for many alert, aware Christians down through the ages.

EMPOWERED TO CONFRONT DEATH

One of the boldest accounts of Christian courage in the face of death comes from the fourth century, from St. Athanasius. He writes,

> A very strong proof of this destruction of death and its conquest by the cross is supplied by a present fact, namely this. All the disciples of Christ despise death; they take the offensive against it and, instead of fearing it, by the sign of the cross and by faith in Christ trample on it as on something dead. Before the divine advent of the Saviour even the holiest of men were afraid of death, and mourned the dead as those who perish. But now that the Saviour has raised His body, death is no longer terrible, but all those who believe in Christ tread it underfoot as nothing, and prefer to die rather than deny their faith in Christ, knowing full well that when they die they do not perish, but live indeed, and become incorruptible through the resurrection. . . . For men who, before they believe in Christ, think death horrible and are afraid of it, once they are converted despise it so completely that they go eagerly to meet it, and themselves become witnesses of the Saviour's resurrection from it. . . . Death has become like a tyrant who has been completely conquered by the legitimate monarch; bound hand and foot as he now is, the passers-by jeer at him, hitting him and abusing him,

no longer afraid of his cruelty and rage, because of the king who conquered him.[14]

Athanasius goes on to say that Christians "deride," "mock," "scorn," and "scoff at" death.[15] We may wonder if this courage is overstated. And yet multiple accounts of martyrdom, even if tinged by hagiography, testify to such acts of courage. It is not, again, that these early Christians felt no fear whatsoever; it is that they mastered their fears in faith and engaged death head-on.

Evidence of the fear that must still have been experienced, if in many cases mastered, comes from *The Martyrdom of Polycarp* (ca. 167), the oldest account of Christian martyrdom outside the New Testament. In this record, Quintus volunteers himself for martyrdom and urges others on toward it. But, says *The Martyrdom*, though Quintus "forced others to go forward," he "then turned coward." Ultimately, Quintus quailed and succumbed to his fear, fleeing death. By contrast, Polycarp and others stayed strong and bravely suffered martyrdom.[16]

More evidence of early Christians bravely facing death comes from the third century. Around the year 251, a plague, perhaps smallpox, raged through the Roman Empire. Such an occurrence has fresh resonance in our postcoronavirus days. Then as now, fear was a prominent reaction to the pandemic. Those who could afford to fled the densely populated cities. The famous physician Galen, for instance, retreated to his country estate until an earlier plague passed. Many pagan priests acted similarly. Later Bishop Dionysius wrote, "At the outset of the disease, they [pagans] pushed the

---

14. Athanasius, *On the Incarnation*, ch. V, para. 27, pp. 57–58.

15. Athanasius, ch. V, para. 27 and 29, pp. 58 and 60.

16. See Mutie, *Death*, 85.

sufferers away and fled from their dearest, throwing them into the roads before they were dead and treating unburied corpses as dirt, hoping thereby to avert the spread and contagion of the fatal disease."[17]

Many Christians, by contrast, took heart in the cross and resurrection and, mastering any fear of death, dared to take care of the sick. Bishop Dionysius again: "Heedless of danger, they took charge of the sick, attending to their every need and ministering to them in Christ. . . . Many, in nursing and curing others, transferred their death to themselves and died in their stead. . . . The best of our brothers lost their lives in this manner, a number of presbyters, deacons, and laymen winning high commendation so that death in this form, the result of great piety and strong faith, seems in every way the equal to martyrdom."[18] Sociologist Rodney Stark thinks it plausible that Christian nursing reduced mortality by as much as two-thirds.[19]

And the surrounding world noticed. Christian mercy and bravery were so evident that by the fourth century, the emperor Julian, who attempted to restore paganism in a Christianizing world, supported the distribution of grain and wine to the poor, complaining that "the impious Galileans [Christians], in addition to their own, support ours, [and] it is shameful that our poor should be wanting our aid."[20]

What was true for the early church remains true for the church today. Cross and resurrection lend courage in the face of death in its many forms, whether by persecution or plague or more mundane

17. Stark, *Triumph of Christianity*, 115.
18. Stark, 117.
19. Stark, 117.
20. Stark, 118.

causes. Christians are called and empowered to confront death bravely, though not hastily and foolhardily. As Stanley Hauerwas writes, "I certainly do not think that Christians are or should be in a hurry to die. . . . Our first task is in living. But we do not live because we are afraid to die, but because we believe our living is a gift that offers us opportunity for service."[21]

THE GIFT OF LIFE

Central to Christian conviction, then, is that life is a gift of God:

> We are not our own creators. Our desire to live should be given shape in the affirmation that we are not the determiners of our life, God is. We Christians are people who must learn to live, as we have learned that life is a gift. We thus live not as if survival is an end in itself, but rather because we know that life allows us the time and space to live in service to God. We should view time not as something to be lived through, nor life as an end in itself, but rather see life as the gift of time enough to love.[22]

It is in the nature of gifts that we are not free to dispose of them as we like. I learned this as a youngster when I wanted the stamp collection of a friend and offered to trade for it a blank-shooting gun my grandfather had given me. Our parents thwarted the transaction as soon as they learned of it. What they knew, and then taught us, was that gifts are "invested with the personality of the donor."[23]

21. Hauerwas, "Introduction," 13.
22. Hauerwas and Bondi, "Memory, Community," 585.
23. Barclay, *Paul and the Gift*, 15.

To trade the gun given to me by my grandfather was to disrespect him and betray a failure in gratitude. Put differently, gifts establish a social bond, and the inappropriate disposal of a gift denies or disparages that bond. As Christian ethicist James Gustafson writes, "What is given is not ours to dispose of as if we had created it, nor ours to use to serve only our own interests, to mutilate, wantonly destroy, and to deprive others of."[24]

God's gift is the gift of life, life in fullness, reconciled to one another and ready to live with and for the other. We receive life as a gift rightly when we do not presume ownership of it but live it in freedom for and with one another. And this is the gift of a life that defeats death in all its Pauline aspects: physical, moral, and eschatological. It grants us vitality and exciting direction for our threescore and ten (or so) years on this earth. Furthermore, it reaches beyond those years to an eternity of unending growth in God, as part of a new heaven and new earth comprehending all creation.

Lastly, it grants us courage in the face of slavery to the fear of death, which otherwise can lead us to readily succumb to political and economic regimes that may, to keep us in line, wield their ultimate threat: death. Psychologists have found that people's attitudes are most friendly to political authoritarianism when they are reminded of the reality of death.[25] Christians are those people who, if true to their convictions and the victory of God in Jesus Christ, should be most impervious to authoritarianism. This was the case with Paul in light of his apocalyptic gospel. Paul saw the law as "ultimately in the service of Death. As Ted Jennings explains, 'Law and death are inextricably bound together. Death is the "or else" of law, without which law does not have the force of law.' Hence, the

24. Cited in Hauerwas and Bondi, "Memory, Community," 586.
25. See Davies, *Nervous States*, 174.

law is described in Rom 8:2 as the 'Law of Sin and Death' (and see 1 Cor 15:55–56). The law requires Death, the threat of Death, or various lesser deaths (imprisonment, impoverishment, enslavement) in order to operate. Because it is fundamentally dependent upon Death (and thereby operates in the service of Death), the law contributes to the spread of Sin."[26]

For Paul, death confronted by Christ had lost its "sting" (1 Cor 15:55), and the law's complicity with death had been unmasked. If we today seek to follow this way, we will notice how neoliberal capitalism uses the force of law to dispossess, impoverish, and incarcerate those whose existence under neoliberalism is most precarious. And we will stand with the precariat, just as Paul stood alongside the "dregs" of his society. There can perhaps be no greater threat to neoliberalism's reign than a church freed from enslavement to the fear of death, trusting in the gifts of abundance unleashed in God's greater economy.

26. Oudshoorn, *Pauline Solidarity*, 235.

EPILOGUE

What does the future hold? If neoliberalism continues unnamed and unimpeded, the future holds gross inequality and precarity for more and more of the population. It holds entrepreneurial selves pitted against one another in a zero-sum game in which fewer and fewer will emerge as "winners." It holds a world in which we are each and all bent toward con artistry and hustling, where already tenuous and frayed social bonds will further disintegrate. It holds a Christianity that exists in increasingly commodified and distorted forms as a capitalistic parasite. And it holds a crippled ecology that will be further degraded and besmirched. In this last regard, some see the atmosphere collapsing as global warming's effects compound and interact disastrously: there will be flooding of coastlines, wars over potable water, more and increasingly worse induced natural disasters, and abandonment of the masses as the wealthy flee to higher and still inhabitable ground and surround themselves with private police forces. I hope this last scenario does not come to pass. But even if it does not, the inheritance we squandrels bequeath to our children and grandchildren clearly is highly depleted and marred—socially, spiritually, politically, and ecologically.[1]

Apocalyptic moments, as I noted in chapter 3, are moments of decision. In them, God's ways are revealed, and a choice is set before us. We may continue deathward—toward a nullity that separates us from God, the source and sustainer of all life—or we may stop, turn around, and head in a new direction. Jesus opened his own ministry in explicitly apocalyptic terms: "The time is fulfilled, and the kingdom of God has come near; repent, and believe in the good news" (Mark 1:15).

"Repent," says Leonard Cohen, "I wonder what they meant?" It is an understandable question. In tired and too prevalent renditions of Christianity, repentance has been trivialized as a matter of giving up alcohol, card playing, movies, colorful language, and so much else that is fun. But Jesus was speaking in and to a riven culture, desperately tired of exile, on a disastrous collision course with the occupying Romans. The culture was driving toward death in more than one way. Jesus announced good news along with—as a part of—repentance. As is often observed, the Greek we translate as "repent" is the verbal form of *metanoia*, which means "to turn around." Centuries before, Moses told the Israelites they had a choice. They could continue deathward, away from the source and sustainer of all life—all good, truth, and beauty—or turn around and choose "life to you and length of days" (Deut 30:19–20). Forget the killjoy "gospel." What Moses and Jesus offered was "abundant life," life in all its fullness (John 10:10).

---

1. For a novel extrapolating a future with neoliberalism taken to its extreme, see Sheldon, *Individutopia*. For a realistic and sobering depiction of what the twenty-first century holds environmentally in light of climate crisis and its cascading effects, see Wallace-Wells, *Uninhabitable Earth*.

All it meant by way of giving up was the relinquishment of whatever heads in the direction of death. So today, repentance for us will mean giving some things up—such as a heedless, exploitative treatment of nonhuman creation. But that is exactly what is killing us, what is bringing destruction to us and our cocreatures and coworshippers. The real good news, the good news of the apocalypse, is not a matter of abandoning joy (or even fun). The real good news is not a matter of scapegoating immigrants or the LGBTQ community. Instead, it is a matter of turning away from a lonely existence, where we can only "look out for number one," toward a community of mutual care and compassion. It is a matter of justice and assistance for the "least" among us. It is a matter of covenant, catholicity, solidarity, and the surmounting of death in all its forms. It is a matter of accepting the gifts of God's economy—an economy that is wider, deeper, and finally richer than that of neoliberal capitalism.

As Kathryn Tanner writes, in God's economy, "my gaining salvation does not exclude anyone else from it. Salvation is not a scarce good to be fought over. Nor is it accessed through partition in ways that suggest others' enjoyment of it might take away from mine."[2] In other words, God's salvation, the salvation of the entire cosmos, is not a zero-sum game. It is not a competition where only one or a few can win. As Tanner goes on to say, this leans directly into and against the neoliberal stream: "Christian beliefs about a shared origin and fate entail, in sum, a refusal of the privatizing of risk and reward at the heart of finance-dominated capitalism. One fails, morally and otherwise, in the company of others. And one gains salvation by God's grace alone."[3]

2. Tanner, *Christianity and the New Spirit*, 204.
3. Tanner, 205.

God's economy, we might say, operates as a kind of agape network. As the philosopher Charles Taylor writes,

> At the heart of orthodox Christianity, seen in terms of communion, is the coming of God through Christ into a personal relation with disciples, and beyond them others, eventually ramifying through the church to humanity as a whole. God establishes the new relationship with us by loving us, in a way we cannot unaided love each other. (John 15: God loved us first.) The lifeblood of this new relation is agape, which can't ever be understood simply in terms of a set of rules, but rather as the extension of a certain kind of relation, spreading outward in a network. The church is in this sense a quintessentially network society, even though of an utterly unparalleled kind, in that the relations are not mediated by any of the historical forms of relatedness: kinship, fealty to a chief, or whatever. It transcends all these, but not into a categorical society based on similarity of members, like citizenship; but rather into a network of ever different relations of agape.[4]

In this network, agape love does not erase or degrade *philia* (friendship) or *eros* (in the sense of romantic love), which are comparatively attractions of like to like. Jesus, after all, had his beloved and especially preferred disciple among his followers, and Paul counseled the married to stay married. But it does remind us that we are called to approach all, preferred and immediately attractive or not, with an agape love that lets the neighbor be the neighbor in all his differentness and strangeness and otherness. Only then can

4. Taylor, *Secular Age*, 282.

we serve his true needs and know our true need of him in turn. This agape network—stretching across barriers of class, ethnicity, nationality, and gender—uniquely witnesses to the oneness or solidarity of humanity, created by the God of Israel and redeemed in Jesus Christ. Despite neoliberalism's insistence, we are not atomized individuals pitted against one another.[5]

A third aspect of God's economy bears mentioning. This economy has a prominent place for priceless and incomparable values over pecuniary or fungible value. Neoliberal capitalism would place a dollar tag on everything it can and ignore or even deplore the rest. Thus as David Graeber notes, the market value "of a commodity is, precisely, the degree to which it can be compared to (and, hence, exchanged for) something else." But when we consider priceless values, including those we might live for and die by, no such comparability and interchangeability are possible: "It might sometimes be possible to argue that one work of art is more beautiful, or one religious devotee more pious than another, but it would be bizarre to ask how *much* more, to say that this monk is five times more pious than that one, or this Rembrandt is twice as lovely as that Monet." Indeed, values in this sense are valuable "because they cannot be compared with anything. They are each considered unique, incommensurable—in a word, priceless."[6] In God's economy, God values each of God's creatures beyond value and rules out our working by any other final accounting.

---

5. For thoughts on networks and conversion, see Campbell, *Deliverance of God*, 130–33.

6. Graeber, *Bullshit Jobs*, 204.

BACK TO THE FUTURE

So what is the future of Christianity, and orthodox Christianity in particular? The church remains divided. But now, as at no point since the Reformation, it sees deeply into profound points of union and communion. Part of this is simply a matter of contrast. As North American culture as a whole has moved further from nominal Christianization, those serious about their faith see how it makes them distinctive. Also, the liturgical movement of the early twentieth century and the ecumenical movement spanning the twentieth century contributed to the recovery and reclamation of the vast riches of the faith in its worship, beliefs, and practices. Practical ecumenism also developed, where Christians encountered each other face-to-face and across divisions, discovering much they held in common. I think here, for example, of the "sidewalk ecumenism" occurring at antiabortion protests. As the surrounding society moves away from nominal Christianity, Christians Protestant, Catholic, and Eastern Orthodox find one another anew and can celebrate a rough agreement on the things that really matter. As historian Brad Gregory adumbrates them, these include "the trinitarian nature of the transcendent creator-God, the natural world as creation, the divinity of Jesus, his bodily resurrection, the reality of the Holy Spirit, original sin, the necessity of faith for salvation, eternal judgment by God, scripture as the revealed word of God, and many aspects of Christian morality."[7]

I don't want to exaggerate the degree of agreement; I would word some of Gregory's affirmations differently myself. Perhaps it is best to say that a broken bridge has been rebuilt from stones found in the ancient, once commonly held tradition. The bridge is wobbly,

7. Gregory, *Unintended Reformation*, 376–77.

and it has its stress points and cracks. But it can and does bear traffic. And with work and attention, it can be made stronger and bear more traffic.

In the late twentieth and early twenty-first centuries, we have seen crucial retrievals, and they are at the same time forward looking. George Lindbeck mused, "We are now better placed than perhaps ever before to retrieve, critically and repentantly, the heritage in the Hebrew scriptures, apostolic writings and early tradition."[8] Among evangelicals, my teacher Robert Webber spearheaded the recovery of appreciation for the early, truly catholic Christian tradition.[9] Later the evangelical InterVarsity Press undertook Thomas Oden's multivolume *Ancient Christian Commentary on Scripture*. Beyond (but not unfriendly to) evangelical confines, modern and vigorous theological commentary has reemerged after being lost for three centuries: witness *The Brazos Theological Commentary on Scripture* and *Belief: A Theological Commentary on the Bible*.

The retrieval of ancient tradition is felicitous on two counts.

First, the tradition is inexhaustible in its treasures and irreplaceable in its Christocentric, apostolic content. We need not reinvent the wheel in terms of beliefs or practices. But we are called to reappropriate the tradition in our own unique modern and postmodern circumstances. The church's living engagement of the ancient but dynamic and alive tradition is not an antiquarian enterprise that asks only what the Bible and the tradition flowing out of it meant in their original context. As Barth said in regard to the Bible, Christian theology (as a practice in service to the church) "does not ask what the apostles and prophets said but what we must say [now] on

8. Lindbeck, "Confession and Community," 9.
9. Webber was prolific, and all of his writing deserves ongoing attention, but the wellhead of his work remains winsomely concentrated in his first book, *Common Roots*.

the basis of the apostles and prophets."[10] Forever returning to our sources, we seek a fresh word for a new day. Apocalypse has happened, but in a sense, it happens again and again.[11]

Second, as different as our circumstances are from those of the early church, the parallels are uncanny and significant. Lindbeck avers that Christians today are "closer to the situation of the first centuries than they've been in more than a millennium and a half."[12] This is worth unpacking at some length.

We may initially observe that our times, more so than at any time since the late fourth century, are not Constantinian times. By *Constantinian*, I do not mean to enter into any debates about just how Christian the historical Constantine was: Was he really converted and, if so, how true a Christian was he? Nor do I mean to globally disparage or dismiss the heritage of the church after Constantine. Rather, I use the term heuristically to connote a situation in which the state and the general culture support and promote Christianity. The early, pre-Constantinian Christians knew that their faith was not widely shared. They knew that they could not depend on cultural customs, let alone judicial and legal institutions, to prop up the church and its work. Accordingly, their mission centered on the church and its liturgical, catechetical, and mutual support systems. Likewise in our day, governmental institutions and culture industries do not broadly support

---

10. Barth, *Church Dogmatics* I/1, 16.

11. David Bentley Hart comments, "One might even say that a tradition exists only as a sustained apocalypse, a moment of pure awakening preserved as at once an ever dissolving recollection and an ever renewed surprise. And so any truly faithful hermeneutical return to the origin of a tradition is the renewal of a moment of revolution, and the very act of return is itself a kind of revolutionary venture that, ever and again, is willing to break with the conventional forms of the fleeting present in order to serve that deeper truth" ("Tradition and Authority," 75–76).

12. Lindbeck, "Confession and Community," 9.

and promote the faith. The church's mission is properly returned to the church, to its culture and its politics.

Relatedly, the hyperpluralism of our culture is not unprecedented. Today, people have hundreds of options about how to live their lives, about what or whom we should ultimately honor and ascribe the highest worth to. But the early Christians knew and moved among a similar pluralism. In the hellenized Roman world in which the apostle Paul evangelized, hundreds of gods were worshiped. The Greek pantheon contained twelve immortals, from Zeus on down. Besides the Greek gods, there were "foreign deities," divinities from Syria, Egypt, Asia Minor, Thrace, and Persia. Then there was a multitude of lesser gods, such as the twin gods Castor and Pollux, favored by sailors; Hecate, a goddess of the crossroads and magic; Eros, the god of love and desire; and Pan, the god of the countryside. In addition, "Various personifications of human qualities, emotions, or desires were also considered worthy of divine honors, including figures like Arete ('virtue'), Eirene ('peace'), Eudaimonia ('prosperity'), Nike ('victory'), Ploutos ('wealth'), or Tyche ('fate' or 'fortune')."[13]

Nor should we neglect to note that since the first century BCE, Rome's emperors were revered as divine. For instance, Julius Caesar was hailed as *divus Iulius* (Julius, the god), and his adopted son Octavian, who would later be known as Caesar Augustus, took the title *divi filius*, or "son of god." Thus people treated the emperor as they did the gods: "they built temples, offered sacrifice, poured out libations, and held festivals, all in his honor."[14]

Pluralism suffused and overflowed in the world of the earliest urban Christians. As the historian Paul Duff summarizes,

13. Duff, *Jesus Followers*, 86.
14. Duff, 87.

Statues and deities appeared in and around the various temples that filled towns and cities, in the streets, in market places, and in town halls. Household deities occupied virtually every home. . . . Besides statues, there were also friezes and mosaics of the gods. They decorated the homes of the elite and appeared both inside and outside public buildings. . . . Finally, anyone interested in the arts or any kind of public entertainment would have encountered the gods over and over again. Virtually every artistic performance would have featured them in one way or another. Choirs sang their praises. Stories of the gods were acted out on stage in theaters across the empire. Literature, both poetry and prose, was chock full of their exploits. Sporting events were not exempt. They were usually connected to festivals in honor of one deity or another.[15]

In short, says Duff, "Wherever he or she turned, the Jesus follower was hedged in by idolatrous practices; it was virtually impossible to avoid them."[16] Of course, we need not today label every alternative to Christianity we meet as simply idolatrous. But the point is that the general culture (or "multiculture") in its pluralism does not support or prop up faith in the triune God: Father, Son, and Holy Spirit. In this regard, our world is like the world of the early Christians.

Finally, we may think our culture, especially in the academy and culture industries, is unique and unprecedented in its presumed atheism—not in its worship of many named and explicit gods but in its rejection of them all. But as N. T. Wright points out, the ancient world was not without this prestigious option. Epicurean philosophy hailed from the third century BCE. Wright emphasizes

15. Duff, 89–90.
16. Duff, 215.

not the Epicurean ultimate pursuit of (moderate) pleasure but its teaching that the gods, if they existed at all, had nothing to do with human or earthly life.[17] Since they ignored us and left us simply to our own devices, so we could ignore them. This same attitude pervades today's statecraft, popular and elite arts and culture, and science (or at least scient*ism*). As the early Christians sometimes met this attitude, so we predominately meet it now.

All this adds up to a commonality between our situation and that of the early Christians that is not often noted—namely, the ineluctability of doubt. We sometimes think that biblical figures and the sainted early Christians held faith without a scintilla of doubt. Even a cursory reading of the Bible shows otherwise: think of the vacillating Israelites in the wilderness, Jonah, Job, Thomas, the Christ-denying Peter, and many others. Matthew tells us explicitly that the apostles themselves were not free of doubt. After traveling and missionizing with Jesus for three years, after the resurrection and frequent meetings with the risen Jesus, the remaining eleven disciples are summoned to a mountaintop by Jesus. "When they saw him," Matthew says, "they worshiped him; *but some doubted*" (Matt 28:17). We are given no hints about the exact nature of this doubt, but surely it consisted not least of an awareness of alternatives.

Should they worship—or assign ultimate worth to—Jesus of Nazareth as the Messiah, the savior of heaven and earth? This is a big ask, especially when we are aware that there are many other candidates for worship and final hope. The disciples were aware of the Pharisean, Sadducean, Essene, zealot, and other options. Matthew says that despite all they had witnessed and experienced at Jesus's side, some apostles lacked certainty and naggingly wondered, "Is this really it? Is he the one in which we should ultimately hope?"

17. See Wright, *History and Eschatology*.

But all eleven soldiered on, doubts in tow. We too, in a hyperpluralistic world, can never be unaware that others imagine and act profoundly differently than we Christians. Faith, however confident, is not certainty in the sense of knowing no alternatives. As Matthew attests, it has been so from the beginning.

In three regards, then—non-Constantinianism, hyperpluralism, and Epicureanism—the world today is rather like, or parallel to, the world of the church before the fifth century. We can accordingly expect both the Bible and early Christian traditions to have renewed, keen, and thoroughgoing resonances for our time and place.

THE CONTOURS OF HOPE, CHALLENGE, FALLIBILITY, AND BEAUTY

There is one glaring difference between the early church followers' circumstances and ours: theirs were pre-Christian and ours are post-Christian. In their world, Christianity had not yet been tried. In ours, many believe Christianity has been tried and found wanting. It is probably impossible to say who had or has the more daunting task. The early Christians, with the empowerment of the Holy Spirit, had to invent Christianity from the ground up. Learning from the mistakes of our predecessors and admitting them as such—which is no small part of what a living tradition does—we have to (empowered by the same Holy Spirit) re-present the faith.

An advantage is that liberalism down to the present day has been partially informed and shaped by Christianity. Consider the virtue of humility. The pre-Christian Romans did not look at humility as a virtue. By contrast, centuries of Christian influence have installed humility as an admirable human trait so that many in our post-Christian society—not least after years of an egomaniacal narcissist in the White House—still regard humility as a desired characteristic of our leaders (and others). Here Christians benefit from a boon of liberalism and can find common cause.

Furthermore, as de-Christianization proceeds, a robust Christianity stands out more and more in its distinctiveness and potentially perceived freshness. As Luke Bretherton puts it, "An age that renders human constructions of religion fragile is at least potentially more open to revelation than a context in which pallid, cultural Christianity has inoculated people against richer, more holistic embodiments of Christian belief and practice."[18]

Neoliberalism attempts to commoditize religions and philosophies, inviting people to choose among them for bits to cobble together into their own individualized package. This often appears under the slogan "spiritual but not religious." Bruce Rogers-Vaughn avers, "The replacement of religion [as institutionalized social and corporate formations] with spirituality is perhaps the most pervasive, effective, and malignant strategy neoliberalism uses to marginalize theology and neutralize its prophetic threat. I intend to be quite clear on this point: *In the context of global neoliberalism, spirituality is not part of the solution. It is part of the problem.*"[19] In such a context, the future of the church depends on resistance to commoditization and "spirituality" as a consumeristic packaging. This means not so much simply verbally protesting but remembering and reembodying the Christian faith in its corporate, material, and spiritual fullness. The Christian faith is not a commodity; it is a way of life. Brad Gregory writes that in Roman Catholicism, Christianity is "first and foremost a shared way of life. Its fundamental mode is not propositional but participatory, not scholarly but sacramental, not individualistic but

18. Bretherton, *Christ and the Common Life*, 250.
19. Rogers-Vaughn, *Caring for Souls*, 77.

interactive."[20] I suggest that the future for all Christianity, not just for Roman Catholicism, lies in just this direction.

In his *Theology and the Spaces of Apocalyptic*, Cyril O'Regan concludes on seven features of the sort of apocalyptic theology he would commend. Two of these are especially relevant to what I am saying here. In regard to the centrality of embodiment, of the corporate and material reenactment of the faith, O'Regan writes that "to be adequate, apocalyptic forms of theology need both to recommend and comment on practices in which vision is made flesh in witness and forms of life that are exemplary."[21] This means pointing to and supporting actual, visible churches that are genuinely and deeply faithful in their corporate, participatory, sacramental, and interactive life.

Each of us will have exemplary, more or less famous communities we may point to. In my case, I think of Dorothy Day and the Catholic Worker movement. I think of the Bruderhof. I think of Englewood Christian Church in Indianapolis. I think of New Monastic communities and of L'Arche, the international collection of communities ministering to and by the mentally disabled.

But with this last, do we come a cropper? It was crushingly revealed in 2020 that L'Arche's founder and leader, the late Jean Vanier, had been involved in a series of sexually abusive relationships. So much admired, he proved to have his failures. This revelation invalidates any misguided idolization and hero-worship we may have had for Vanier. But it does not invalidate the work of L'Arche. The Christian response to failure is repentance and the relinquishment of hero-worship. This repentance was modeled by the ministry, which itself investigated and disclosed Vanier's offenses, then

---

20. Gregory, *Unintended Reformation*, 363.
21. O'Regan, *Theology and the Spaces*, 128.

set to work imagining how it might prevent future such offenses. At their best, says George Lindbeck, Jews and Christians have "perhaps unparalleled" resources to be "maximally critical of their own communities without disloyalty, as is abundantly illustrated by their own Scriptures."[22] From Jacob/Israel to Peter with the keys to the kingdom, the Scriptures show their characters with their flaws and foibles.

Have done, then, with hero-worship and admiration first and foremost of the famous. Look instead to a church or churches you know well and to everyday examples of faithfulness there. Think of the couple sixty years married, still delighting in one another and God. Think of the neighborhood church that stood up against injustice to immigrants. Think of your own church's quiet victories of endurance in the face of setbacks and opposition. The point is not, again, to idolize or stop our vision on these exemplars, which all have clay feet. It is to treat them as icons we look *through* to see and focus on Jesus. It is Jesus alone who lived without sinning. It is Jesus alone who never fails. It is Jesus alone through whom all creation was made and redeemed.

In Jesus we find unsurpassed admirability and unsurpassed beauty. And beauty brings me to the second of O'Regan's relevant features of apocalypticism. O'Regan writes that a commendable apocalyptic theology (lived as well as articulated) attempts to

22. Lindbeck, "Gospel's Uniqueness," 247. Perhaps once a year, every church should read Hans Urs von Balthasar's "Casta Meretrix," touring Scripture's depiction of Israel and the church as the very fallible "chaste whore." For a beautiful novelistic depiction of saintliness and fallenness, see Frederick Buechner's *Godric*, which features a protagonist with no less a flaw than brother-on-sister incest. For a probing examination of the limitations and weak points of Christian character development, see Winner, *Dangers of Christian Practice*. Finally, for an anguished cri de coeur concerning the church's current brokenness, see Bell, "Trump as Mirror."

persuade by the power and beauty of its vision so that apocalyptic has an affinity with "aesthetic forms of theology."[23]

"The practice of evangelism," Bryan Stone writes, "could very much use a reconnection to beauty. And when it's reconnected to beauty, we may find that evangelism becomes more a work of art, embodiment, and imagination than an exchange of information or a technology designed to secure results."[24] Stone insightfully argues that leading with beauty (while not dismissing truth or goodness) is worthwhile for two reasons, to which I will add a third.

First, beauty calls us to live out of control: "For we are in no more a position to control or contain beauty than we are to control or contain a sunset. True beauty always grasps us rather than our grasping it. And though we might recognize it, reflect it, even participate in it, beauty somehow always exceeds us and defies our attempts to contain it."[25] Above all, Christians want to point beyond themselves to God in Jesus Christ. This is a God we did not invent and do not control. We participate in and reflect the triune, overflowing life of this God as a community, but we never "contain" this God. Beauty points to the transcendent, something (or Someone) beyond even itself. How appropriate, then, that we know God as the true and ultimate end or goal of beauty, which always exceeds us.

Second, "beauty, once discovered, demands to be reproduced and shared."[26] Who, when she hears a beautiful song, does not at once want to tell a friend about it? Who, coming upon cranes in flight with their dulcet calls, does not want to point them out to a companion? For that matter, who, coming across a loving, warm

---

23. O'Regan, *Theology and the Spaces*, 128.
24. Stone, *Evangelism after Pluralism*, 117. See also Gibbs, *Apologetics after Lindbeck*, 41–50.
25. Stone, *Evangelism after Pluralism*, 118.
26. Stone, 120.

community, does not want to invite in someone else? Beauty promotes or induces sharing and connection to others. We are intended for community and harmony with all creation. Nothing more winsomely or effectively moves us toward that end than beauty.

Third, and relatedly, beauty is compelling but not coercive. God, by Christian accounting, does not overwhelm us and crush us with imperatives. God is interested in our genuine love; God woos but does not rape. God stoops to the human level and accommodates human finitude and fallibility, culminating in the cross where God hangs broken and dying to take on human sin and defeat death. In these senses, God "evangelizes" not through implacable propositions, hemming us in with logical arguments, but through participating in our very earthly life and offering costly love. And there is something unsurpassably beautiful about this. Especially in a post-Constantinian, post-Christian world, we can no longer—to our own as well as to others' benefit—attempt to coerce faith. We can, however, live it in a way that we hope will be beautiful and so draw others to it. The early church, itself literally unable to coerce participation, recognized this as appropriate to the very ways and character of God. Consider these examples:

> For God does not compel, since force is hateful to God, but He provides for those who seek. (Clement of Alexandria)

> [God works] by means of persuasion . . . [God] does not use violent means to obtain what he desires. (Irenaeus)

> Religion must be defended not by killing but by dying, not by violence but by patience. (Lactantius)[27]

27. All three quoted in Kreider, *Patient Ferment*, 120.

THE SIGNIFICANCE OF GATHERING

In this spirit, I want to conclude with some words on a mundane, basic practice of Christians that we too easily overlook and take for granted. I mean our act of gathering to worship.[28] To get out of bed on a Sunday morning, to go to be with other Christians for prayer and praise, seems simple and relatively insignificant. But it is not. The coronavirus pandemic, for all its destruction, reminded us how precious and crucial it is to gather: to see and touch others, to consume together the body and blood of Christ—that is, the *life* of Christ—on a regular basis, and to be constituted as the body of Christ. Sheltering separately at home, we were deprived of this physical meeting and its power. We missed it and longed for it.

No wonder, when we stop to think about it. We are creatures made to worship. I do not mean just the hour or two when we put our butts in pews, though that is crucial. I mean worship in the sense of ascribing worth to something or someone. This we are constantly doing, in or outside a church, synagogue, or mosque. We gather in stadiums and rise for the national anthem, and so we ascribe worth. We gather in supermarkets and malls, and so we ascribe worth to shopping and consumerism. We gather in restaurants and camping grounds, and so we ascribe worth to good food and time away closer to creation. Thus theologian Philip Kenneson rightly asserts that

---

28. Though I here have chosen to focus on the practice of gathering, there are other promising angles from which to consider Christian resistance to neoliberalism. One of them is true and deep friendship. In this regard, see May, *Friendship in an Age of Economics*; and the final chapter of my *A Peculiar People*, "The Church as a Community of Friends," 187–211.

"human gatherings always involve worship, and worship always implicates human gatherings."[29]

Furthermore, our gatherings are not simply expressive of individual needs, wants, and self-understanding. Rather, gatherings are formative: "Because human beings are social creatures, when they gather together they inevitably presuppose and reinforce much about the shape, meaning, and purpose of the world that they understand themselves to inhabit. Indeed, all human gatherings are inevitably formative, not least because such gatherings construct an imaginative landscape (a 'world') within which all future action and reflection upon it will take place. People come to have a world as they gather together and share stories about the shape and meaning of that world, as well as their place and role within it."[30]

Of course, some gatherings are more intensive and formative than others. The marines in boot camp are more profoundly affected and formed as particular sorts of persons than the thrill-seekers who congregate for a few hours in an amusement park:

> The difference in relative impact among gatherings is the result of many factors, including such things as their frequency (how often these gatherings take place), their stability over time (whether a relatively stable group of persons gather), their intended scope (how much of human life this gathering seeks to influence and order), their type and intensity of interaction fostered (the kind of social relations those gathering engage in and the potentially formative influence of that intimacy), and the willingness on the part

29. Kenneson, "Gathering," 53.
30. Kenneson, 55.

of those gathered to be caught up in vision of the world being presupposed and reinforced by that gathering.[31]

The church's worship is central in all these ways: it gathers at least weekly; roughly the same group of people gather from week to week in the local church; worship's scope, the stories it tells and the symbols it corporately employs, encompasses the entire cosmos; the interaction is maximally intensive in that the people gather as a new, first family, as first and foremost siblings in Christ; and the church is composed of people who eagerly seek to be formed in the image of Christ, who have been drawn by the beauty of the Christian apocalyptic story and not coerced to reluctantly participate. In short, this assembly, the *ekklesia*, "is understood to be the primary context in which disciples of Jesus Christ learn the skills, convictions, and dispositions that animate its life in the world."[32] In gathered worship, the church "opens itself up to receive the proper orientation to all that is, in order that it might live in *that* world in ways consonant with the reign of the triune God."[33]

Intensive as Christian worship might be, it is not insular. In gathering, the church becomes "visible and addressable, opening itself up to being probed and criticized, not only by God, but also by the world." That is as it should be. "The *ekklesia*, as an imperfect anticipation of what God desires for all creation, seeks to conceal neither its faithfulness nor its unfaithfulness, its own sinfulness—as well as have its sinfulness named by others," and that "is itself a form of faithful witness to this God and this God's work."[34]

31. Kenneson, 57–58.
32. Kenneson, 59.
33. Kenneson, 65.
34. Kenneson, 66.

Nor at this juncture should we forget the apocalyptic nature of the gospel we proclaim and seek to have shape our lives. Apocalyptic, remember, always looks first to God's initiative. The church does not claim to bring in the kingdom on its own but witnesses to God's actions in Christ. A constant awareness of this reality militates against hero-worship and any

> romantic exaggeration of the ethical capability of Christians. . . . In other words, unless Christians know that their ethical activity is essentially an anticipation of that greater reality of God's coming kingdom, they cannot but wonder about the futility of their efforts in view of the overwhelming structures of evil and suffering in the world. And unless Christians know that there task is to establish nothing but beachheads of the kingdom of God in this world, then not only the sheer magnitude of the ethical task will suffocate them, but also their frequent inability to measure ethical progress will stifle them. . . . For only God himself will be able to complete the work that he began in us in Christ (Phil. 1:6).[35]

Centered and formed in gathered worship, the church recognizes and celebrates Christ's kingship over all that is and will be, which is itself a political act. Furthermore, the church local—and certainly catholic—gathers people across gender, age, ethnicity, and class. There are no privileged parking places or seating plans. The custodian may serve on the church board alongside the CEO. Crossing and including all classes, the church is again uniquely political.

Beyond that, Christians may work with others outside the church who hold, at points, overlapping interests and aims. In the face of

35. Beker, *Paul's Apocalyptic Gospel*, 86–87.

neoliberal capitalism, that should include work to limit the market's reach and reembed it in and subordinate it to the public weal. It should also include a forthright recognition of class conflict and the fact that neoliberalism radically favors the wealthy's welfare at the expense of the less wealthy and the poor. This last, in a world where policy debate tries to ignore or deny class, will incite complaints that Christians are promoting class warfare. But as William Cavanaugh wryly observes, that is like accusing firemen of arson because they keep showing up at burning houses.[36] The church can and should brave nonviolent conflict, not least in its concern for the neediest among us.

In naming neoliberalism, we name a—if not the—preeminent power and principality of our time. The world and not just the church can do better. There is a far more noble freedom, freedom *for* as well as freedom *from*, to be won. There is a truer justice to be desired. There is a better peace to be secured. Christians live by apocalyptic hope, but that hope can make a difference not just tomorrow. It can make a difference today.

36. Cavanaugh, *Field Hospital*, 28.

ACKNOWLEDGMENTS

This book is the product of several friendships. I am grateful to friends who took the time to review a nearly final draft of the manuscript and offer thorough critiques. These friends are Mike Budde, Bill Cavanaugh, Stan Hauerwas, and Steve Long.

Two other friends offered much. Bill Greenway, besides gently keeping me jealous of his home in Austin, Texas (truly the "live music capital" of the world), closely engaged two chapters at a crucial stage. B. J. Heyboer encouraged and supported me—on a daily basis—in the writing from to the beginning to the end, let me know how her fellow pastors would "hear" what I wrote, and counseled on potential endorsers.

I also want to thank my new friends, Ryan Hemmer at Fortress for his adept developmental editing and the editors at Scribe Inc. for their meticulous copyediting.

I dedicate this book to Scott Young. It has been thirty-some years since we first met and immediately initiated a deep and still unended conversation on matters cultural, theological, and political—and on the ups and downs of our everyday lives. We leap at the chance for person-to-person meetings but are mostly separated by the distance between Chicago and Los Angeles. I am grateful to Scott for his constancy in our hour-long phone calls two or three times a month.

Finally, I must once again note the role played by my closest friend and companion, Sandy Clapp. For more than forty years,

ACKNOWLEDGMENTS

Sandy has been with me through thick and thin, modeling faithfulness, grounding me in God's good creation, sustaining me with delicious meals, humoring me in my quirks, birthing and parenting our excellent daughter, and lifting me again and again into what can only be called joy.

BIBLIOGRAPHY

Abram, David. *Becoming Animal: An Earthly Cosmology*. New York: Vintage, 2010.

————. *The Spell of the Sensuous: Perception and Language in a More-Than-Human World*. New York: Vintage, 2017.

Ahn, Ilsup. *Just Debt: Theology, Ethics, and Neoliberalism*. Waco, TX: Baylor University Press, 2017.

Allison, Dale C., Jr. *Constructing Jesus: Memory, Imagination, and History*. Grand Rapids: Baker Academic, 2010.

Ammeson, Jane. "An Interview with Milton Friedman." *Chicago Life*, June 1, 2006. https://tinyurl.com/y7dhtl9o.

Anderson, Braden P. *Chosen Nation: Scripture, Theopolitics, and the Project of National Identity*. Theopolitical Visions. Eugene, OR: Cascade, 2012.

Athanasius. *On the Incarnation*. Translated and edited by a Religious of CSMV. Crestwood, NY: St. Vladimir's Seminary Press, 1944.

Augustine. *Confessions*. Modern English version. Grand Rapids: Revell, 2008.

Babie, Paul, and Michael Trainor. *Neoliberalism and the Biblical Voice: Owning and Consuming*. Routledge Studies in Religion 60. New York: Routledge, 2018.

Badiou, Alain. *Saint Paul: The Foundation of Universalism*. Translated by Ray Brassier. Cultural Memory in the Present. Stanford, CA: Stanford University Press, 2003.

Balmer, Randall. *Thy Kingdom Come: How the Religious Right Distorts Faith and Threatens America*. New York: Basic, 2006.

Balthasar, Hans Ur von. "Casta Meretrix." In *Explorations in Theology*, vol. 2, *Spouse of the Word*, 193–288. San Francisco: Ignatius, 1991.

Banner, Michael. *The Ethics of Everyday Life: Moral Theology, Social Anthropology, and the Imagination of the Human*. Oxford: Oxford University Press, 2014.

Baptist, Edward E. *The Half Has Never Been Told: Slavery and the Making of American Capitalism*. New York: Basic, 2016.

Barclay, John M. G. *Paul and the Gift*. Grand Rapids: Eerdmans, 2015.

Barth, Karl. *Church Dogmatics* I/1. Edited by G. W. Bromiley and T. F. Torrance. Translated by G. W. Bromiley. Edinburgh: T&T Clark, 1975.

———. *Church Dogmatics* II/1. Edited by G. W. Bromiley and T. F. Torrance. Translated by T. H. L. Parker et al. Edinburgh: T&T Clark, 1957.

———. *Church Dogmatics* IV/1. Edited by G. W. Bromiley and T. F. Torrance. Translated by G. W. Bromiley. Edinburgh: T&T Clark, 1956.

———. *Church Dogmatics* IV/2. Edited by G. W. Bromiley and T. F. Torrance. Translated by G. W. Bromiley. Edinburgh: T&T Clark, 1958.

Bauckham, Richard. *Living with Other Creatures: Green Exegesis and Theology*. Waco, TX: Baylor University Press, 2011.

Beiner, Ronald. *What's the Matter with Liberalism?* Berkeley: University of California Press, 1992.

Beker, J. Christiaan. *Paul's Apocalyptic Gospel: The Coming Triumph of God*. Minneapolis: Fortress, 1982.

———. *Paul the Apostle: The Triumph of God in Life and Thought*. Philadelphia: Fortress, 1980.

Belcher, Jodi L. A. "'Discerning the Body' at the Apocalyptic Standpoint: A Feminist Engagement with Martyn's Thought." In *Apocalyptic and the Future of Theology: With and Beyond J. Louis Martyn*, edited by Joshua B. Davis and Douglas Harink, 236–263. Eugene, OR: Cascade, 2012.

Bell, Daniel M., Jr. "Trump as Mirror for the Church: Death and Despair, Hope and Resurrection of the Church." *Religions* 11, no. 3 (2020): 107. https://doi.org/10.3390/rel11030107.

Benjamin, Walter. "Capitalism as Religion." In *Selected Writings*, vol. 1, *1913–1926*, edited by Marcus Bullock and Michael W. Jennings, 288–291. Cambridge, MA: Belknap Press of Harvard University Press, 1996.

Block, Fred, and Margaret R. Somers. *The Power of Market Fundamentalism: Karl Polanyi's Critique*. Cambridge, MA: Harvard University Press, 2014.

Bonhoeffer, Dietrich. *Discipleship*. Dietrich Bonhoeffer Works 4. Translated by Barbara Green and Reinhard Krauss. Minneapolis: Fortress, 2001.

Borg, Marcus J. *Jesus: A New Vision*. San Francisco: Harper & Row, 1987.

Bossy, John. *Christianity in the West, 1400–1700*. Oxford: Oxford University Press, 1985.

Bourne, Randolph S. "The State." In *War and the Intellectuals: Collected Essays 1915–1919*, 65–104. Indianapolis: Hackett, 1964.

Bretherton, Luke. *Christ and the Common Life: Political Theology and the Case for Democracy*. Grand Rapids: Eerdmans, 2019.

Buechner, Frederick. *Godric*. San Francisco: HarperSanFrancisco, 1980.

Campbell, Alexia Fernández. "CEOs Made 287 Times More Money Last Year Than Their Workers Did." Vox, June 26, 2019. https://tinyurl.com/y38neqql.

Campbell, Douglas A. *The Deliverance of God: An Apocalyptic Rereading of Justification in Paul.* Grand Rapids: Eerdmans, 2009.

———. *Paul: An Apostle's Journey.* Grand Rapids: Eerdmans, 2018.

———. *Pauline Dogmatics: The Triumph of God's Love.* Grand Rapids: Eerdmans, 2019.

Cary, Phillip. *The Meaning of Protestant Theology: Luther, Augustine, and the Gospel That Gives Us Christ.* Grand Rapids: Baker Academic, 2019.

Cavanaugh, William T. *Being Consumed: Economics and Christian Desire.* Grand Rapids: Eerdmans, 2008.

———. *Field Hospital: The Church's Engagement with a Wounded World.* Grand Rapids: Eerdmans, 2016.

———. *Migrations of the Holy: God, State, and the Political Meaning of the Church.* Grand Rapids: Eerdmans, 2011.

———. *Theopolitical Imagination: Discovering the Liturgy as a Political Act in an Age of Global Consumerism.* London: T&T Clark, 2002.

———. *Torture and Eucharist: Theology, Politics, and the Body of Christ.* Challenges in Contemporary Theology. Malden, MA: Blackwell, 1998.

Charles, Mark, and Soong-Chan Rah. *Unsettling Truths: The Ongoing, Dehumanizing Legacy of the Doctrine of Discovery.* Downers Grove, IL: InterVarsity, 2019.

Clapp, Rodney. *Families at the Crossroads: Beyond Traditional and Modern Options.* Downers Grove, IL: InterVarsity, 1993.

———. "Free for What?" Review of *Freedom*, by Jonathan Franzen. *Christian Century*, November 2, 2010, 36–37.

———. *Johnny Cash and the Great American Contradiction: Christianity and the Battle for the Soul of a Nation.* Louisville, KY: Westminster John Knox, 2008.

———. "The Monkhood of All Believers: On Monasticism Old and New." In *To Be Welcomed as Christ: Paving the Way for a Hospitable Evangelicalism*, edited by Nicholas Scott-Blakely. Eugene, OR: Cascade, forthcoming.

———. *New Creation: A Primer on Living in the Time between the Times*. Eugene, OR: Cascade, 2018.

———. *A Peculiar People: The Church as Culture in a Post-Christian Society*. Downers Grove, IL: InterVarsity, 1996.

Coakley, Sarah. *God, Sexuality, and the Self: An Essay "On the Trinity."* Cambridge: Cambridge University Press, 2013.

Collins, John J. *What Are Biblical Values? What the Bible Says on Key Ethical Issues*. New Haven, CT: Yale University Press, 2019.

Cox, Harvey. *The Market as God*. Cambridge, MA: Harvard University Press, 2016.

Davies, J. P. *Paul among the Apocalypses? An Evaluation of the "Apocalyptic Paul" in the Context of Jewish and Christian Apocalyptic Literature*. Library of New Testament Studies. London: T&T Clark, 2016.

Davies, William. "Introduction to Economic Science Fictions." In *Economic Science Fictions*, edited by William Davies, 1–28. London: Goldsmiths, 2018.

———. *The Limits of Neoliberalism: Authority, Sovereignty and the Logic of Competition*. Revised ed. Theory, Culture and Society. Los Angeles: Sage, 2017.

———. *Nervous States: Democracy and the Decline of Reason*. New York: W. W. Norton, 2018.

Day, Keri. *Religious Resistance to Neoliberalism: Womanist and Black Feminist Perspectives*. Black Religion / Womanist Thought / Social Justice. New York: Palgrave Macmillan, 2016.

Dean, Robert J. *For the Life of the World: Jesus Christ and the Church in the Theologies of Dietrich Bonhoeffer and Stanley Hauerwas*. Eugene, OR: Pickwick, 2016.

de Boer, Martinus C. "Cross and Cosmos in Galatians." In *Paul, Theologian of God's Apocalypse: Essays on Paul and the Apocalypse*, 90–105. Eugene, OR: Cascade, 2020.

———. *The Defeat of Death: Apocalyptic Eschatology in 1 Corinthians 15 and Romans 5*. Journal for the Study of the New Testament Supplement Series 22. London: T&T Clark, 1988.

Deneen, Patrick J. *Why Liberalism Failed*. Politics and Culture. New Haven, CT: Yale University Press, 2018.

deSilva, David A. *Honor, Patronage, Kinship and Purity: Unlocking New Testament Culture*. Downers Grove, IL: IVP Academic, 2000.

Donoghue, Emma. *Room*. New York: Back Bay, 2011.

Dorrien, Gary. *Social Democracy in the Making: Political and Religious Roots of European Socialism*. New Haven, CT: Yale University Press, 2019.

Duff, Paul B. *Jesus Followers in the Roman Empire*. Grand Rapids: Eerdmans, 2017.

Duggan, Lisa. *The Twilight of Equality? Neoliberalism, Cultural Politics, and the Attack on Democracy*. Boston: Beacon, 2003.

Du Mez, Kristin Kobes. *Jesus and John Wayne: How White Evangelicals Corrupted a Faith and Fractured a Nation*. New York: Liveright, 2020.

Eastman, Susan Grove. "Apocalypse and Incarnation: The Participatory Logic of Paul's Gospel." In *Apocalyptic and the Future of Theology: With and Beyond J. Louis Martyn*, edited by Joshua B. Davis and Douglas Harink, 165–182. Eugene, OR: Cascade, 2012.

Eggemeier, Matthew T. *Against Empire: Ekklesial Resistance and the Politics of Radical Democracy*. Theopolitical Visions. Eugene, OR: Cascade, 2020.

Eggemeier, Matthew T., and Peter Joseph Fritz. *Send Lazarus: Catholicism and the Crises of Neoliberalism*. New York: Fordham University Press, 2020.

Ehrenreich, Barbara. *Natural Causes: An Epidemic of Wellness, the Certainty of Dying, and Killing Ourselves to Live Longer.* New York: Twelve, 2018.

Episcopal Church. *Book of Common Prayer.* New York: Church Publishing, 2006.

Fountain, Ben. *Billy Lynn's Long Halftime Walk.* New York: Ecco, 2012.

Franzen, Jonathan. *Freedom.* New York: Farrar, Straus and Giroux, 2010.

Fraser, Steve. *The Age of Acquiescence: The Life and Death of American Resistance to Organized Wealth and Power.* New York: Basic, 2015.

Garvey, Jon. *God's Good Earth: The Case for an Unfallen Creation.* Eugene, OR: Cascade, 2019.

Gaventa, Beverly Roberts. *Our Mother Saint Paul.* Louisville, KY: Westminster John Knox, 2007.

Gibbs, Jeremiah. *Apologetics after Lindbeck: Faith, Reason, and the Cultural-Linguistic Turn.* Eugene, OR: Pickwick, 2015.

Graeber, David. *Bullshit Jobs: A Theory.* New York: Simon & Schuster, 2018.

————. *Debt: The First 5,000 Years.* Updated and expanded ed. Brooklyn, NY: Melville House, 2014.

————. *The Utopia of Rules: On Technology, Stupidity, and the Secret Joys of Bureaucracy.* Brooklyn, NY: Melville House, 2016.

Gregory, Brad S. *The Unintended Reformation: How a Religious Revolution Secularized Society.* Cambridge, MA: Belknap Press of Harvard University Press, 2012.

Griffiths, Paul J. *Christian Flesh.* Encountering Traditions. Stanford, CA: Stanford University Press, 2018.

Hargaden, Kevin. *Theological Ethics in a Neoliberal Age: Confronting the Christian Problem with Wealth.* Theopolitical Visions. Eugene, OR: Cascade, 2018.

Harink, Douglas. *Paul among the Postliberals: Pauline Theology beyond Christendom and Modernity*. Eugene, OR: Wipf and Stock, 2003.

Hart, David Bentley. *Atheist Delusions: The Christian Revolution and Its Fashionable Enemies*. New Haven, CT: Yale University Press, 2009.

———. *That All Shall Be Saved: Heaven, Hell and Universal Salvation*. New Haven, CT: Yale University Press, 2019.

———. "Tradition and Authority: A Vaguely Gnostic Meditation." In *The Idea of Tradition in the Late Modern World: An Ecumenical and Interreligious Conversation*, edited by Thomas Albert Howard, 57–77. Eugene, OR: Cascade, 2020.

———. "What Lies Beyond Capitalism?" *Plough Quarterly* (Summer 2019): 30–38.

Harvey, David. *A Brief History of Neoliberalism*. Oxford: Oxford University Press, 2005.

Hauerwas, Stanley. "The Church and Liberal Democracy: The Moral Limits of a Secular Polity." In *A Community of Character: Toward a Constructive Christian Social Ethic*, 72–86. Notre Dame, IN: University of Notre Dame Press, 1981.

———. "The Church in a Divided World: The Interpretative Power of the Christian Story." In *A Community of Character: Toward a Constructive Christian Social Ethic*, 89–110. Notre Dame, IN: University of Notre Dame Press, 1981.

———. "How Risky Is *The Risk of Education*? Random Reflections from the American Context." In *The State of the University: Academic Knowledges and the Knowledge of God*, Illuminations/Theory and Religion, 45–57. Malden, MA: Blackwell, 2007.

———. "Introduction: The Scope of This Book." In *Against the Nations: War and Survival in a Liberal Society*, 1–22. Minneapolis: Winston, 1985.

———. "Leaving Ruins: The Gospel and Cultural Formations." In *The State of the University: Academic Knowledges and the Knowledge of God*, Illuminations/Theory and Religion, 33–44. Malden, MA: Blackwell, 2007.

Hauerwas, Stanley, and Richard Bondi. "Memory, Community, and the Reasons for Living: Reflections on Suicide and Euthanasia." In *The Hauerwas Reader*, edited by John Berkman and Michael Cartwright, 577–595. Durham, NC: Duke University Press, 2001.

Holland, Tom. *Dominion: How the Christian Revolution Remade the World*. New York: Basic, 2019.

Hopkins, Gerard Manley. "Inversnaid." In *Poems and Prose*, selected and edited by W. H. Gardner, 50–51. New York: Penguin, 1979.

Horrell, David G. *The Bible and the Environment: Towards a Critical Ecological Biblical Theology*. Biblical Challenges in the Contemporary World. London: Routledge, 2014.

———. *Solidarity and Difference: A Contemporary Reading of Paul's Ethics*. 2nd ed. Cornerstones. London: Bloomsbury T&T Clark, 2016.

Hoskyns, Edwyn Clement, and Francis Noel Davey. *Crucifixion-Resurrection: The Pattern of Theology and Ethics in the New Testament*. London: SPCK, 1981.

Immerwahr, Daniel. *How to Hide an Empire: A History of the Greater United States*. New York: Farrar, Straus and Giroux, 2019.

Jardine, Murray. *The Making and Unmaking of Technological Society: How Christianity Can Save Modernity from Itself*. Grand Rapids: Brazos, 2004.

Jennings, Willie James. *Acts*. Belief: A Theological Commentary on the Bible. Louisville, KY: Westminster John Knox, 2017.

———. *The Christian Imagination: Theology and the Origins of Race*. New Haven, CT: Yale University Press, 2010.

Keesmaat, Sylvia C., and Brian J. Walsh. *Colossians Remixed: Subverting the Empire*. Downers Grove, IL: InterVarsity, 2004.

———. *Romans Disarmed: Resisting Empire, Demanding Justice*. Grand Rapids: Brazos, 2019.

Kenneson, Philip. "Gathering: Worship, Imagination, and Formation." In *The Blackwell Companion to Christian Ethics*, 1st ed., edited by Stanley Hauerwas and Samuel Wells, 53–67. Malden, MA: Blackwell, 2004.

Klein, Naomi. *The Shock Doctrine: The Rise of Disaster Capitalism*. New York: Metropolitan, 2007.

———. *This Changes Everything: Capitalism vs. the Climate*. New York: Simon & Schuster, 2014.

Kotsko, Adam. *Neoliberalism's Demons: On the Political Theology of Late Capital*. Stanford, CA: Stanford University Press, 2018.

Kreider, Alan. *The Patient Ferment of the Early Church: The Improbable Rise of Christianity in the Roman Empire*. Grand Rapids: Baker Academic, 2016.

LaMothe, Ryan. *Care of Souls, Care of Polis: Toward a Political Pastoral Theology*. Eugene, OR: Cascade, 2017.

Leshem, Dotan. *The Origins of Neoliberalism: Modeling the Economy from Jesus to Foucault*. New York: Columbia University Press, 2016.

———. "What Did the Ancient Greeks Mean by *Oikonomia*?" *Journal of Economic Perspectives* 30, no. 1 (Winter 2016). tinyurl.com/ebcj3vux.

Levenson, Jon D. *The Love of God: Divine Gift, Human Gratitude, and Mutual Faithfulness in Judaism*. Library of Jewish Ideas. Princeton, NJ: Princeton University Press, 2016.

Levering, Matthew. *Engaging the Doctrine of Marriage: Human Marriage as the Image and Sacrament of the Marriage of God and Creation*. Eugene, OR: Cascade, 2020.

Lindbeck, George A. "Confession and Community: An Israel-Like View of the Church." In *The Church in a Postliberal Age*, edited by James J. Buckley, 1–9. Radical Traditions. Grand Rapids: Eerdmans, 2002.

———. "The Gospel's Uniqueness: Election and Untranslatability." In *The Church in a Postliberal Age*, edited by James J. Buckley, 223–252. Radical Traditions. Grand Rapids: Eerdmans, 2002.

Linzey, Andrew, and Tom Regan, eds. *Animals and Christianity: A Book of Readings*. Eugene, OR: Wipf and Stock, 1990.

Lohfink, Gerhard. *Does God Need the Church? Toward a Theology of the People of God*. Translated by Linda M. Maloney. Collegeville, MN: Michael Glazier, 1999.

Long, D. Stephen. *Augustinian and Ecclesial Christian Ethics: On Loving Enemies*. Lanham, MD: Lexington, 2018.

———. *Truth Telling in a Post-truth World*. N.p.: GHBEM, 2019.

Lumet, Sidney, dir. *Network*. Los Angeles: Metro-Goldwyn-Mayer, 1976.

Lynerd, Benjamin T. *Republican Theology: The Civil Religion of American Evangelicals*. Oxford: Oxford University Press, 2014.

MacIntyre, Alasdair. *After Virtue: A Study in Moral Theory*. 2nd ed. Notre Dame, IN: University of Notre Dame Press, 1984.

———. *Whose Justice? Which Rationality?* Notre Dame, IN: University of Notre Dame Press, 1988.

Malina, Bruce J. *The New Testament World: Insights from Cultural Anthropology*. Atlanta: John Knox, 1981.

Marshall, Peter, and David Manuel. *The Light and the Glory: 1492–1793*. Revised and expanded ed. Grand Rapids: Revell, 2009.

Martyn, J. Louis. "Apocalyptic Antinomies." In *Theological Issues in the Letters of Paul*, 111–123. Nashville: Abingdon, 1997.

———. "Christ and the Elements of the Cosmos." In *Theological Issues in the Letters of Paul*, 125–140. Nashville: Abingdon, 1997.

———. *Galatians*. Anchor Yale Bible 33A. New Haven, CT: Yale University Press, 1997.

May, Todd. *Friendship in an Age of Economics: Resisting the Forces of Neoliberalism*. Lanham, MD: Lexington, 2012.

McCarraher, Eugene. *The Enchantments of Mammon: How Capitalism Became the Religion of Modernity*. Cambridge, MA: Belknap Press of Harvard University Press, 2019.

Middleton, J. Richard. *A New Heaven and a New Earth: Reclaiming Biblical Eschatology*. Grand Rapids: Baker Academic, 2014.

Mirowski, Philip. *Never Let a Serious Crisis Go to Waste: How Neoliberalism Survived the Financial Meltdown*. London: Verso, 2014.

Moo, Douglas. *The Epistle to the Romans*. New International Commentary on the New Testament. Grand Rapids: Eerdmans, 1996.

———. *The Letter to the Romans*. 2nd ed. New International Commentary on the New Testament. Grand Rapids: Eerdmans, 2018.

Mountford, Peter. *A Young Man's Guide to Late Capitalism*. New York: Mariner, 2011.

Mutie, Jeremiah. *Death in Second-Century Christian Thought: The Meaning of Death in Earliest Christianity*. Eugene, OR: Pickwick, 2015.

Newson, Ryan Andrew. *Radical Friendship: The Politics of Communal Discernment*. Minneapolis: Fortress, 2017.

Niebuhr, H. Richard. *Christ and Culture*. New York: Harper Torchbooks, 1951.

O'Donovan, Oliver. *The Desire of the Nations: Rediscovering the Roots of Political Theology*. Cambridge: Cambridge University Press, 1996.

O'Regan, Cyril. *Theology and the Spaces of Apocalyptic*. Milwaukee: Marquette University Press, 2009.

Orwell, George. "Notes on Nationalism." In *Essays*, edited by John Carey, 865–884. New York: Everyman's Library, 1968.

Oudshoorn, Daniel. *Pauline Solidarity: Assembling the Gospel of Treasonous Life*. Paul and the Uprising of the Dead 3. Eugene, OR: Cascade, 2020.

Perelman, Michael. *The Invention of Capitalism: Classical Political Economy and the Secret History of Primitive Accumulation*. Durham, NC: Duke University Press, 2000.

Pinches, Charles R. *A Gathering of Memories: Family, Nation, and Church in a Forgetful World*. Eugene, OR: Wipf and Stock, 2006.

Polanyi, Karl. *The Great Transformation: The Political and Economic Origins of Our Time*. 1944. Reprint, Boston: Beacon, 2001.

Pope Francis. *Evangelii Gaudium: The Joy of the Gospel*. Vatican City: Libreria Editrice Vaticana, 2013.

Powers, Richard. *The Overstory*. New York: W. W. Norton, 2018.

Raschke, Carl. *Neoliberalism and Political Theology: From Kant to Identity Politics*. Edinburgh: University of Edinburgh Press, 2019.

Reno, R. R. *Return of the Strong Gods: Nationalism, Populism, and the Future of the West*. Washington, DC: Regnery Gateway, 2019.

Rogers-Vaughn, Bruce. *Caring for Souls in a Neoliberal Age*. New Approaches to Religion and Power. New York: Palgrave Macmillan, 2016.

Rutledge, Fleming. *Advent: The Once and Future Coming of Jesus Christ*. Grand Rapids: Eerdmans, 2018.

Safdie, Benny, and Josh Safdie, dirs. *Uncut Gems*. Los Angeles: A24, Elara Pictures, IAC Films, Scott Rudin Productions, Sikelia Productions, 2019.

Satia, Priya. *Empire of Guns: The Violent Making of the Industrial Revolution*. New York: Penguin, 2018.

Scafaria, Lorene, dir. *Hustlers*. Los Angeles: Gloria Sanchez Productions, Annapurna Pictures, Nuyorican Productions, STX Films, 2019.

Scott, James C. *Seeing like a State: How Certain Schemes to Improve the Human Condition Have Failed*. Yale Agrarian Studies. New Haven, CT: Yale University Press, 1998.

Shain, Barry Alan. *The Myth of American Individualism: The Protestant Origins of American Political Thought*. Princeton, NJ: Princeton University Press, 1994.

Sheldon, Joss. *Individutopia*. Self-published, 2018.

Siedentop, Larry. *Inventing the Individual: The Origins of Western Liberalism*. Cambridge, MA: Belknap Press of Harvard University Press, 2014.

Slobodian, Quinn. *Globalists: The End of Empire and the Birth of Neoliberalism*. Cambridge, MA: Harvard University Press, 2018.

Smith, James K. A. *Awaiting the King: Reforming Public Theology*. Cultural Liturgies 3. Grand Rapids: Baker Academic, 2017.

———. *Desiring the Kingdom: Worship, Worldview, and Cultural Formation*. Cultural Liturgies 1. Grand Rapids: Baker Academic, 2009.

———. *The Fall of Interpretation: Philosophical Foundations for a Creational Hermeneutics*. 2nd ed. Grand Rapids: Baker Academic, 2012.

———. *Imagining the Kingdom: How Worship Works*. Cultural Liturgies 2. Grand Rapids: Baker Academic, 2013.

Solnit, Rebecca. *A Paradise Built in Hell: The Extraordinary Communities That Arise in Disaster*. New York: Viking, 2009.

Song, Robert. *Covenant and Calling: Towards a Theology of Same-Sex Relationships*. London: SCM, 2014.

Spaulding, Henry Walter, III. *The Just and Loving Gaze of God with Us: Paul's Apocalyptic Political Theology*. Eugene, OR: Wipf and Stock, 2019.

Springs, Jason A. *Toward a Generous Orthodoxy: Prospects for Hans Frei's Postliberal Theology*. Eugene, OR: Wipf and Stock, 2010.

Stark, Rodney. *The Triumph of Christianity: How the Jesus Movement Became the World's Largest Religion*. New York: HarperOne, 2011.

Stone, Bryan. *Evangelism after Christendom: The Theology and Practice of Christian Witness*. Grand Rapids: Brazos, 2007.

———. *Evangelism after Pluralism: The Ethics of Christian Witness*. Grand Rapids: Baker Academic, 2018.

Sunkara, Bhaskar. *The Socialist Manifesto: The Case for Radical Politics in an Era of Extreme Inequality*. New York: Basic, 2019.

Tanner, Kathryn. *Christianity and the New Spirit of Capitalism*. New Haven, CT: Yale University Press, 2019.

Taubes, Jacob. *Occidental Eschatology*. Translated by David Ratmoko. Cultural Memory in the Present. Stanford, CA: Stanford University Press, 2009.

———. *The Political Theology of Paul*. Translated by Dana Hollander. Cultural Memory in the Present. Stanford, CA: Stanford University Press, 2004.

Tawney, R. H. *Religion and the Rise of Capitalism*. 1926. Reprint, London: Verso, 2015.

Taylor, Charles. *A Secular Age*. Cambridge, MA: Belknap Press of Harvard University Press, 2007.

Tonstad, Linn Marie. *Queer Theology*. Cascade Companions. Eugene, OR: Cascade, 2018.

Wallace, Mark I. *When God Was a Bird: Christianity, Animism, and the Reenchantment of the World*. New York: Fordham University Press, 2019.

Wallace-Wells, David. *The Uninhabitable Earth: Life after Warming*. New York: Tim Duggan, 2019.

Walsh, Brian J., Marianne B. Karsh, and Nik Ansell. "Trees, Forestry, and the Responsiveness of Creation." *CrossCurrents* 44, no. 2 (Summer 1994): 149–162. https://www.jstor.org/stable/24460092.

Waters, Brent. *Just Capitalism: A Christian Ethic of Economic Globalization*. Louisville, KY: Westminster John Knox, 2016.

Webber, Robert E. *Common Roots: A Call to Evangelical Maturity*. Grand Rapids: Zondervan, 1978.

Weber, Max. *The Protestant Ethic and the "Spirit" of Capitalism and Other Writings*. 1905. Reprint, New York: Penguin, 2002.

Whitehead, Andrew L., and Samuel L. Perry. *Taking America Back for God: Christian Nationalism in the United States*. New York: Oxford University Press, 2020.

Williams, Rowan. "The Body's Grace." 1989. Anglican Church of Canada, 2010. https://tinyurl.com/y526etyb.

Wilson, Julie A. *Neoliberalism*. Key Ideas in Media and Cultural Studies. New York: Routledge, 2018.

Winner, Lauren F. *The Dangers of Christian Practice: On Wayward Gifts, Characteristic Damage, and Sin*. New Haven, CT: Yale University Press, 2018.

Wolfe, Alan. *Whose Keeper? Social Science and Moral Obligation*. Berkeley: University of California Press, 1989.

Wolin, Sheldon S. *Politics and Vision: Continuity and Innovation in Western Political Thought*. Expanded ed. Princeton, NJ: Princeton University Press, 2004.

Wright, N. T. *History and Eschatology: Jesus and the Promise of Natural Theology*. 2018 Gifford Lectures. Waco, TX: Baylor University Press, 2019.

———. *Paul and the Faithfulness of God*. Book 2. Minneapolis: Fortress, 2013.

———. *Surprised by Hope: Rethinking Heaven, the Resurrection, and the Mission of the Church*. New York: HarperOne, 2008.

Yarbrough, O. Larry. *Not like the Gentiles: Marriage Rules in the Letters of Paul*. Atlanta: Scholars, 1985.

Zaleski, Carol. *Otherworld Journeys: Accounts of Near-Death Experiences in Medieval and Modern Times*. New York: Oxford University Press, 1987.

Ziegler, Philip G. *Militant Grace: The Apocalyptic Turn and the Future of Christian Theology*. Grand Rapids: Baker Academic, 2018.

Zizioulas, John D. *Being as Communion: Studies in Personhood and the Church*. Crestwood, NY: St. Vladimir's Seminary Press, 1985.

INDEX

INDEX

INDEX

INDEX